There May Be Trouble Ahead

A Practical Guide to Effective Patent Asset Management

Lex van Wijk

The Scarecrow Press, Inc.
Lanham, Maryland • Toronto • Oxford
2005

SCARECROW PRESS, INC.

Published in the United States of America
by Scarecrow Press, Inc.
A wholly owned subsidiary of
The Rowman & Littlefield Publishing Group, Inc.
4501 Forbes Boulevard, Suite 200, Lanham, Maryland 20706
www.scarecrowpress.com

PO Box 317
Oxford
OX2 9RU, UK

British Library Cataloguing in Publication Information Available

Library of Congress Cataloging-in-Publication Data

Wijk, Lex van, 1959–
   There may be trouble ahead : a practical guide to effective patent asset
management / Lex van Wijk.
      p. cm.
   Includes bibliographical references and index.
   ISBN 0-8108-5292-6 (pbk. : alk. paper)
   1. Patents—United States. I. Title.

T339.W665 2005
608.773—dc22

                                                   2004029809

Jointly dedicated to the memories of my father
and of Ernst Pfeiffer, a fine patent colleague

Endorsements

"Commercialisation of IP is now considered essential for success in business and indeed of the economies of nations. Trade agreements take into account IP issues. This book provides an insight into the business world from an author who has experienced the development of IP awareness from its confined area of a few years ago to its broad recognition today. This is essential reading for managers and directors of companies with an interest in technological development and for patent professionals who now must not only obtain IP rights for clients but guide those clients on the appropriate use of it.

This work does not resort to platitudes as many texts do and is therefore easily followed and its teachings remembered. An exercise in plain English. Much of what is taught is available elsewhere. This text puts it together for the benefit of the reader. The work does reveal the patent attorney background of the author but that is its strength, not a weakness."—Malcolm Royal, Phillips Ormonde & Fitzpatrick

"Lex's practical guide provides a wonderful overview of the elements of patent asset management. It covers an amazing amount of ground in a relatively small number of pages. It provides excellent insights by someone who obviously has a lot of experience in the area. I would definitely recommend it as an addition to any intellectual asset management library."—Harry J. Gwinnell, vice president and chief intellectual property counsel, Cargill Incorporated

"This short book by Lex van Wijk is described as being a practical guide, and it lives up to this description. Many books and articles on patent asset management describe elaborate mathematical methods for calculating cash valuations of patent portfolios, and often seem to be out of touch with reality. This book gives a clear and simple approach to the evaluation of inventions and patents, and encourages companies to consider whether their patenting strategy really matches their business and R&D strategies. I thoroughly recommend this book to all patent attorneys working in industry, as well as to managers in need of an introduction to this subject."—Dr. Philip Grubb, author of *Patents for Chemicals, Pharmaceuticals and Biotechnology*

Contents

Foreword

There was a time when commercialization of innovation was the preserve of multinational corporations. With some exceptions, only these corporations had the resources and knowledge to take an invention from conception to product sale. In 1968, I was employed as licensing officer of the Australian Commonwealth Scientific and Industrial Research Organization, and even in that well-revered organization it was almost impossible to interest industry in developing new things they were working on.

All that has changed. We are now the "knowledge-based society." Governments encourage us to be innovative. But how can we take that innovation through to the marketplace?

At first sight, commercialization appears to be a fairly straightforward art. But the more one looks at the question, the more one appreciates that this is not so. How does one interest others in a good idea? Only the inventor does not require convincing. Others may be led to the water, but how do you get them to drink? It is not merely a question of funds. It requires technical appreciation, understanding of markets, and above all, dedication.

Lex van Wijk has many years of invaluable experience within the multinational business world, and we are privileged that he is passing on that experience in this book. *There May Be Trouble Ahead* is essential reading for managers and directors of companies with an interest in technological development and for patent professionals who now must not only obtain IP rights for their clients but also guide those clients on the appropriate use of the protection they obtain.

This work does not resort to platitudes as many texts do and is therefore easily understood and its teachings remembered. An exercise in plain English. Much of what is taught is available elsewhere. This text puts it together for the benefit of the reader. The work does reveal the patent attorney background of the author but that is its strength, not a weakness.

Malcolm Royal
Managing Partner of Phillips Ormonde &
Fitzpatrick Australia
President of Honour of the Fédération Internationale
des Conseils en Propriété Industrielle
President of The Institute of Patent and Trade Mark
Attorneys Australia

Preface

These are awkward times for many in-house patent professionals. In the past, patent assets may not have been given the attention in their company that they deserve. Patent professionals may have experienced difficulty in convincing the business of the strategic relevance of the company's patent portfolio and related activities. Quite recently, however, things have started to change rapidly. Top management is starting to realize that patent assets can bring additional revenues to their company, which is important because profit margins are increasingly under pressure in today's global economy. If the Chief Executive Officer (CEO) or Chief Financial Officer (CFO) has not yet knocked on your intellectual property (IP) director's door, expect this to happen. Their expectations regarding the performance of patent portfolios will be high. Top management will increasingly expect intellectual property rights (IPRs) to be managed as a business, turning, where possible, a traditionally expensive patent operation into a source of profits. For many patent departments the heat is on, and there may be trouble ahead. This may especially be the case because of the increasing workloads of patent departments in general and the fact that the role of a patent department traditionally has been a relatively reactive one. Moreover, many patent departments have yet to establish effective patent asset management tools. This is not criticism but merely an observation.

The same also applies to patent professionals in private practice, though in a less direct way. Small and medium-sized enterprises are also starting to realize that patent assets are becoming increasingly important business tools. These enterprises also wish to exploit their patent assets to a greater extent and expect their patent portfolios to be managed efficiently and cost-effectively. They want well-defined patent strategies tailored to their business needs. This particularly applies to start-up companies in the fields of biotechnology, software, and telecommunications, where well-defined patent strategies and properly managed patent portfolios have become essential to attract investors. Moreover, because of the knowledge economy and the ongoing globalization, various national governments, but also the

European Commission and the World Intellectual Property Organization (WIPO), are starting to urge small and medium-sized companies to pay more attention to patenting, patent strategies, and the management of their patent portfolios. However, increasing workloads and the absence of effective tools to manage patent assets will also make it difficult for patent professionals in private practice to meet their clients' increasing demands and expectations. For them, there may be trouble ahead, too.

These developments are not passing fads but are expected to continue because of the ongoing globalization and increasingly aggressive competition. Therefore, patent professionals cannot shy away from these troubles. In today's business environment these troubles need to be faced and dealt with and the sooner the better. This book aims to provide a set of tools that will enable patent professionals from industry as well as private practice to deal with these troubles in a successful manner. The tools are relatively simple, and their successful implementation does not depend on the size of a company's patent portfolio. The tools are considered key for managing a company's patent assets in an effective but relatively simple manner, with emphasis on management and simplicity. Patents are a complex subject, and it is easy to lose oneself in interesting and important details. This book, however, is about the big managerial picture. It focuses on the fundamental elements of effective patent asset management that need to be understood and put in place. Therefore, matters such as case law, national patent law requirements, guidelines for drafting claims, litigation strategies, etc., though most important, will not be discussed. Besides, others are undoubtedly more knowledgeable on such matters. Further, this book is not exhaustive on the subject, but again that is intentional. It is hoped that it will stimulate patent professionals to take an active approach to this exciting and increasingly important business area.

Why share these tools? We are entering an era in which the sharing of knowledge and technology will be crucial to companies. The "not invented here" attitude will belong to the past. By sharing knowledge and technology, not only the companies involved will benefit, but also society. The same principle applies to the sharing of knowledge regarding the management of patent assets, and that should not be too difficult to do for patent professionals. After all, that is what patents are all about. They provide people a monopoly right for a limited time, and in turn those people share knowledge regarding an invention with the public, thus enabling society to benefit from the invention, too.

Readers are welcome to provide comments. They can be e-mailed to l.vanwijk@vereenigde.nl.

Acknowledgments

This book is primarily based on my experiences within industry at Royal Dutch Shell, Burmah Castrol, and Siemens AG. As is inevitable, various insights and tools that are described in this book have been inspired and influenced by work from and/or discussions with colleagues, consultants, and others.

The books of Stephen Glazier and H. Jackson Knight on patent strategy awoke my interest in the field of patent asset management. The teachings of Karl-Erik Sveiby on knowledge-based assets have had a lasting influence on many of my ideas relating to the management of patent assets. Apart from Karl-Erik, I have also had stimulating discussions with Pat Sullivan, Baruch Lev, Bruce Burton, and Sam Khoury, all acknowledged experts in their own right.

At Siemens AG, the analytic approach, including the combination of certain matrices as developed by Dr Hans Goslowsky (now a manager at Software for Intellectual Property GmbH) and Rolf Ohmke, has been very inspiring. I would like to thank my former Siemens colleagues Mark Schulze and Wolfgang Mocker for the enjoyable discussions on portfolio management.

I thank my former colleagues at Burmah Castrol, in particular Julie Miles, Pauline Lewis, Peter Beaney, Tony Clayton-Hathway, and last but not least, Malcolm Davies, for creating such an enjoyable work atmosphere, which stimulated me to explore the various ideas described in this book.

I am grateful to Jeremy Ridge for suggesting to put my ideas in writing.

To Ashley Ralston, thanks for assisting me with some of the graphs. Thanks to Jolanda van der Toorn for her initial help with the table of contents and the index and her assistance in coordinating the typesetting process.

Special thanks to Vereenigde for sponsoring the typesetting of the book.

Bob Vanderhye earns my special thanks for his sound advice, enabling me to publish the book as it is.

To Jacob Eisenberg and Ton van der Straaten, my great gratitude for providing useful comments on the manuscript.

My greatest thanks to Richard Crack, with whom I have had the privilege of working for several years. Without his patience and stimulating and encouraging comments, this book would simply not have been written.

Likewise, my dearest thanks goes out to my loved ones, my wife, Angèle, and our two girls, Emmeline and Sylvie, for their love, patience, and support in allowing me time to work on this book.

1
Effective Patent Asset Management

For technology-based companies, patent assets are becoming increasingly important. Their presence or absence can make or break such companies. It is for this reason that patent asset management is becoming a core responsibility within these companies.

One of the major tasks within the field of patent asset management is to develop a patent strategy that ensures a company's patent portfolio is of a high quality and of the right size and shape, that it contains patent assets that really support the company's business and research and development (R&D) goals.

Effective patent asset management should therefore ensure that strengths and weaknesses of a company's patent portfolio and opportunities and threats vis-à-vis competitors are identified or anticipated in a timely manner, enabling proper action to be taken, if required. It should make sure that a company's patent assets are managed in such a way that the company has the best possible patent position in the marketplace and that these assets really contribute to the company's future success, if not survival.

Elements of Effective Patent Asset Management

If one wishes to manage a company's patent assets in an effective manner, at least the following elements need to be covered:

- Patent strategy
- Alignment of strategies
- Invention evaluation
- Measurement of IP performance
- A new IP culture
- Business endorsement

Chapter 1

Patent Strategy

A patent strategy is a framework of decision-making processes and procedures that ought to ensure that the patent activities of a company are tailored to the company's business needs. It should make sure that the company will have a competitive edge over the competition and that it can operate without major threats and disputes in the marketplace. It should be clear from the patent strategy what the strategic objectives of the company's patent portfolio and patent activities are and how these strategic objectives will be realized.

Alignment of Strategies

To ensure that a company's patent activities are tailored to its business needs, the company's patent strategy should be aligned with the company's business and R&D strategies. To establish this, a company should first know where it currently stands and where it wishes to go. In other words, first the company's business environment and business vision must be known. Subsequently, the company must select those patent activities that will assist the company in establishing its corporate goals in the best possible manner, and these patent activities need to be emphasized in the company's patent strategy.

Invention Evaluation

Having a set of criteria to use in evaluating inventions will facilitate the alignment of strategies and enable a company to distinguish the strategically important inventions from the less important inventions. This allows one to focus on the inventions that really matter to a company and to avoid unnecessary costs and wasted time, since patent professionals could prioritize their activities in a proper way. Further, such set of evaluation criteria will enable a company to mine its patent portfolio in an efficient manner.

Measurement of IP Performance

To determine the extent to which a company has aligned its patent strategy with its business and R&D strategies, one must periodically measure the performance of the company's patent assets. In that way, the company can, for instance, obtain an understanding of the use and impact of its patent assets in the marketplace, the growth and renewal of its patent portfolio, and the return on investment in these assets. Possible areas of potential risk, particular trends, and areas of necessary change in the patent portfolio and related activities can thus be identified in a timely manner, and if required, appropriate action can be taken.

A New IP Culture

In today's knowledge-based economy, patent assets play an increasingly important role, and companies' expectations regarding the performance of these assets and related management are growing. Can patent professionals meet these expectations? In principle they can, but it will generally take a great effort and strong commitment, especially since the role of patent professionals traditionally has been a relatively reactive one. To be successful, patent professionals need to establish a new IP culture, one with greater emphasis on value creation and extraction.

Business Endorsement

Since patent assets are becoming increasingly important strategic business tools, any decision regarding these assets needs to be an informed business decision, taken in close consultation with the business and R&D functions. For patent asset management to be successful, a strong commitment is required throughout the company, and the company's efforts in this area should be fully supported by top management.

The interaction of these six elements is schematically shown in figure 1.1.

Conclusion

To ensure that a company's patent assets are managed in an effective manner, the company should have a properly defined patent strategy that is aligned with its business and R&D strategies. To establish successfully alignment of strategies, the company's business environment and business vision need to be known; the company's inventions

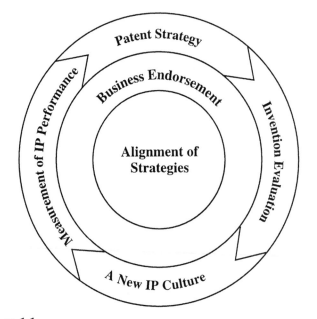

Figure 1.1
Effective Patent Asset Management—the PatStrat™Method

need to be evaluated in a consistent manner; the performance of the
company's IP should be measured periodically; patent professionals
need to develop and implement a new IP culture; and top management
should support the company's activities in the field of patent asset
management. The first five of these elements will each be discussed in
detail in one of the following chapters, whereas business endorsement,
the element that is fundamental to the interoperability of the other five
elements, will be discussed in more general terms throughout the
book.

2
Developing a Patent Strategy

The term "patent strategy" has become somewhat of a buzzword. Not only is it commonplace in the IP world, but it is also making significant inroads into corporate boardrooms. The reason for this is that patents and intellectual property rights in general are becoming increasingly important to companies. This is for example shown by the continuing growth in the number of patent applications in industry. In today's global economy, patent assets are strong business tools to obtain or maintain a competitive advantage. Many companies consider them vital for the future prosperity of their business. It is therefore surprising that not very much has been written on the subject, although there exist some books that are essential reading.[1]

Generally, a patent strategy can be defined as a framework of decision-making processes and procedures that should ensure that a company's patent activities support the company's current business and that they will assist the company in realizing its business vision. A patent strategy should ensure that a company's patent assets add value to the company's bottom line, whereas at the same time it should enable a company to operate commercially without major patent threats and disputes in the marketplace. If required, a patent strategy may need to be developed in respect of each business area, technology area, or individual technology.

Objectives of Patent Protection

When developing a patent strategy, the first question to be answered is what is it that one wants to achieve by filing a patent application for a particular invention or series of inventions.

Generally, the three main reasons to seek patent protection are:

- Exclusivity to prevent imitation by others
- Licensing to generate royalty income
- Freedom of action or design, that is, to be able to use one's own technology or that of others through cross-licensing

Additional reasons, though normally of less relevance, are:

- A sense of achievement/prestige for employees, thereby creating an atmosphere wherein the development of inventions by employees is encouraged
- Use as a sales aid or marketing tool, for instance, by putting on a package "Patent Pending"
- Developing a reputation for being an innovative company, enabling the recruitment of skilled people

Moreover, patents are generally seen as insurance for protecting a company's R&D investment. They may give the company the chance to recoup its investment in R&D.

When properly managed, patent assets can provide companies a competitive advantage in their respective markets. However, since patents are relatively expensive, the cost of filing should always be weighed against the potential benefit of patent protection. Generally, patent applications should be filed for inventions that increase a company's competitive edge.

The Foundation of a Patent Strategy

A technology-based company that wants to develop a proper patent strategy needs to address and consider at least the following elements:

- Education program
- Confidentiality program
- Monitoring patent activities of third parties
- Report of inventions
- Review of inventions
- Filing program
- Ownership
- Enforcement function
- Infringement of patents of third parties
- Patent assets audits
- Licensing
- Due diligence
- Oddball inventions or strategic misfits

The extent to which a company needs to look into each of these elements depends on factors such as market size and growth, market share, and the relevance of technology and patents in the marketplace. However, independent of these factors, every technology-based company is recommended to look into these elements because they form the foundation of an appropriate patent strategy.

Each of these elements will now be discussed in more detail.

Education Program

Business and R&D personnel should appreciate and understand what patents are and how they can be used to provide a competitive advantage. It is therefore advisable to put an internal education program in place to bring all business and R&D personnel up to an acceptable base level of knowledge regarding patent rights and intellectual property rights in general. Such a program could, for instance, be an integral part of an induction process for all new business and R&D personnel. Also, a program of periodic reminder sessions for existing staff might prove useful.

Confidentiality Program

Internal rules should be established to ensure that no journal articles are written or conference presentations made without prior clearance by a patent professional. In that way, possible loss of potential patent protection could be prevented.

When confidential information needs to be disclosed to another party, for instance, during joint research or development, it is recommended to put a confidentiality agreement in place requiring the other party to keep the information received in confidence.

In case it is decided to develop a particular invention further with another company, it is not only recommended to have a confidentiality agreement in place between the two companies, but also recommended to have filed a patent application covering the invention before starting the joint development. In this way, any potential future dispute about the ownership of the invention can be avoided.

Monitoring Patent Activities of Third Parties

Patent applications are normally published eighteen months after the filing of the first application and are a very useful source of technical information.

To obtain an understanding of competitors' R&D efforts and intentions, it is recommended to monitor their patent activities. In addition, it may help to identify research direction, especially when entering a new technology area.

By monitoring the patent activities of competitors, duplication of R&D efforts can possibly be avoided. On the other hand, it may draw a company's attention to new technologies in respect of which the company may wish to create a patent position itself, thereby possibly creating cross-licensing opportunities. It may also enable a company to select potential partners with which to collaborate.

Moreover, potential infringement risks can be identified at an early stage, and filing oppositions in those countries where the filing of oppositions is possible can be considered, or a decision can be made as to what other action is needed to respond to a competitor. It is, however, advised to monitor only others' patent activities in technology areas that are of interest to a company or that could become of interest in the future.

A company could consider including in an internal patents information database a section that would give an overview of all the patent documents that have been published in the previous month in the technology areas that are relevant to the company. Such a section could be updated at least once a month.

Report of Inventions

General

Newly conceived inventions should be reported to a patent professional as early as possible. This will enable a patent professional to look after the patents interest of a company locally and, if desired, globally. Patent professionals should be contacted in respect of any sort of new technology, be it a new product, manufacturing process, package design, business method, or software program.

It is very difficult to retrieve a position if an application has not been filed or an invention has been published prematurely. Therefore, good communication between patent professionals and business and R&D personnel is crucial at the reporting stage.

Once an invention has been reported, it is very important to make sure that patent professionals are kept informed about any further work on the original invention, thus enabling them to seek patent protection also for further modifications and improvements.

An important question to be considered at this stage is whether patents of other companies should preclude or modify research in a particular technology area. The answer to this question depends on the circumstances. First, a company could well develop technology outside the claims of the patent in question, which technology may be patentable as such. Second, a company may develop an improved technology, possibly giving rise to a selection invention on the basis of which a cross-license opportunity may be created.

Inventor Encouragement

It is good practice to present inventors a plaque of the first page of the European or U.S. patent granted covering their inventions. This brings about a sense of achievement for the inventors. In addition, the introduction of a program of cash incentives, for example, a one-time payment, may be considered to encourage employees to disclose ideas for inventions.

U.S. Companies

In the United States a patent is granted to the first-to-invent (rather than the first-to-file); therefore it is essential that inventors keep records of all their experiments and work from the time the invention is conceived.

Such record of an invention should be dated and signed by all inventors and two witnesses who are not the inventors but fully understand the idea behind the invention.

Best practice is to use laboratory notebooks for that purpose. The absence of such practice, and thus the lack of evidence to prove a date of invention, may result in losing the right to the invention to a third party that has developed an identical invention independently.

After the General Agreement on Tariffs and Trade (GATT) it has also become possible in the United States to prove a date of invention for an invention originating in another country. Therefore, it is also advisable to use laboratory notebooks for experimental work outside the United States in technology areas that are also of high commercial interest in the United States.

Review of Inventions

General

Once reported, inventions need to be reviewed for their merits. To this end, the reported inventions need to be reviewed by both patent professionals and business and R&D personnel to ensure that inventions are identified that may yield patents of value to the business in question.

The first question to be answered at this stage is whether the invention should be patented.

In general, the filing of a patent application should only take place when there is a perceived value in doing so. Protection should therefore be sought for those inventions that are considered to be patentable and according to business and R&D personnel have commercial potential or other benefit to the business.

Hence, in respect of each reported invention a decision needs to be made whether patent protection should be sought, the invention should be kept as a trade secret, or its subject matter should be disclosed to the public for freedom of action purposes.

In chapter 4, the evaluation of inventions is discussed in detail.

Further Experimental Work Required

When an invention is reported and only a limited amount of technical or experimental information is available, it needs to be decided whether it is necessary to carry out further experimental work to ensure that a useful scope of protection can be obtained. If patents are too narrow, even if they cover the commercial products of a company, they may permit a competitor to circumvent the patent and enter the market with a slightly different product. If patents are too broad, without proper support/substantiation, they may leave room for competitors to develop improvements for which they could obtain patent protection themselves, thereby possibly creating cross-licensing opportunities. In addition, patents that have been granted and of which the scope of protection is too broad may be difficult, if not impossible, to enforce. On the other hand, a broad but weak patent application could possibly be useful as a marketing tool or may have nuisance value vis-à-vis a company's competitors.

Generally, to obtain a strong and broad patent some experimental work needs to be carried out. So, if a company wants to obtain a useful exclusive position in respect of a new technology/product that is patentable, at least a fair amount of research effort needs to be carried out regarding the technology/product, to ensure that the objective of establishing useful exclusivity can be realized.

Patent Protection versus Trade Secrets

Usually, it is preferred to seek patent protection for a patentable invention with commercial potential rather than keep it as a trade secret. However, in certain circumstances it might be preferable to keep the new technology concerned as a trade secret, for instance if

- The invention is not patentable.
- Too much know-how would be disclosed.
- The invention is of little commercial interest.
- The patent can easily be circumvented.
- The invention cannot be properly policed.

It is, however, an absolute requirement that the trade secret is not known to others. It is therefore advisable to label trade secret documents as confidential. Further, it is an important task to control who has access to the information and what they are allowed to do with it.

Keeping inventions as trade secrets is not without risk. It may well be that a patent can be obtained by a third party for the subject matter of the company's trade secret, possibly creating the obligation to pay license fees to that third party.

Freedom of Action

It may well be that the primary interest of the business is to enjoy freedom to work the invention, that is, to preclude others from obtaining patent protection for the same invention at a later stage. This so-called freedom of action or design objective can be established by publishing the invention, for instance anonymously in *Research Disclosure*, a U.S. journal that is published every month.

Series of Related Inventions

As indicated before, it is very important to obtain a proper under-standing of the scope of the technical concept of the invention. By carrying out a range of experiments, a company may be in the position to recognize possible modifications (e.g., alternative embodiments) and improvements of the original invention.

This is especially of importance when developing a new business line. In such cases it needs to be considered what the objective is of developing the new technology involved. For instance, does a company want to create a completely new, unique product to be the main, if not only, player in the market, or does it just want to create a me-too product? In the former case, patent protection seems necessary, whereas in the latter it may not be warranted.

Such considerations are important since the filing of patent appli-cations on modifications and improvements might prove to be very useful, because in that way a long-lived technology can be protected even after its basic coverage has expired. Moreover, a competitor is more likely to be successful in circumventing one particular patent than a series of patent applications relating to the same technical concept.

Yet another reason to protect modifications and improvements of an invention is that a competitor may try to patent an improvement over one of a company's inventions once he has learned about it after its publication. In that way, the competitor may be in the position to force a company to give it a cross-license.

It is therefore very important to make an informed decision whether to patent further modifications and improvements of an invention.

Selection Invention over a Dominating Third Party Patent

By filing a patent application covering an improvement (selection invention) over a dominating third party patent, a company may possibly create a cross-license opportunity, since the third party may wish to work within the company's patent.

Creating a Patent Portfolio

To establish an appropriate exclusive position, a portfolio of patent assets usually includes patents with both broad and narrow scopes of protection, that is, covering both basic inventions and selection inventions over the basic concept.

Software and Related Inventions

For many companies, business methods are an integral part of their business, and these methods are believed to be becoming increasingly important in industry in general. Many of the business methods today are based on software applications, and since there is an international trend that business methods and software as such can be patented, companies must look into the possibility of patenting business methods and the software on which these methods are based. In this way, patent protection for a company's unique services to customers could possibly obtained, and copying of these services by competitors could be prevented. Business and R&D personnel are therefore advised to contact patent professionals at an early stage when a new or improved software-based business method or software program has been developed.

Design Protection

In case it would not be possible to obtain valid patent protection for a device such as some sort of package, the possibility of obtaining design protection should be considered.

Patent Searches

Once it has been decided that an invention should be protected, it is advisable to carry out a novelty search before a patent application is drafted. In this way, a company can avoid filing patent applications for inventions that are not patentable. In addition, if the invention is patentable, any relevant prior art can be considered from the start, thus improving the chances of obtaining a strong patent. However, it may not be necessary to carry out such a search in cases where the prior art is well known to the inventor.

Filing Program

First Filing

When the decision has been made to seek patent protection for an invention, a patent application needs to be drafted, and it must be decided where the patent application will be first filed, taking into consideration national patent law requirements. As to the United States, it is worth noting that it is possible to file provisional patent applications at the United States Patent and Trademark Office (USPTO). These provisional patent applications have various advantages.[2] Further, in respect of important inventions originating outside the United States it is worth considering filing simultaneously a first application in the jurisdiction concerned, for example, at the European Patent Office (EPO), and a provisional patent application at the USPTO. Such practice may provide a substantial advantage if one were to get involved in interference proceedings before the USPTO at a later stage.

Foreign Filing

Some time after the first filing of a patent application (normally after nine or ten months) a decision needs to be made whether it is justified to seek patent protection elsewhere and, if so, the countries where further patent applications need to be filed should be identified.

A company with global presence needs to consider in which countries patent protection would or could provide a further competitive edge. Since patent rights do normally provide protection for a period of twenty years after filing, it is important to consider in addition to the present countries of interest also those countries in which potential business growth is expected during that period of twenty years.

Since patents give a company the right to prevent others from performing the invention covered by the patent, it may in certain circumstances even be prudent to file patent applications in countries where a company is not active but where one of its competitors is manufacturing products that may affect a company's global business.

Foreign filing, however, is expensive and should therefore normally be done only in the countries where there is a potential for recouping the costs incurred. It is also of importance to take the local enforcement climate for patents into consideration when deciding where to foreign file a patent application.

A company that wishes to use its patents mainly for defensive purposes could limit its foreign filing program to those countries where the company has a business interest and intends to work the invention. On the other hand, a company that wants to use its patents for more offensive purposes could decide to extend its foreign filing program to the countries where competitors have a business interest, as well as those countries where both the company and its competitors may have a business interest at some stage during the lifetime of the patent right in question.

Generally, patent applications should be more broadly filed in respect of important inventions than for less important inventions. It is therefore clear that foreign filing should take place in those countries where the invention is likely to be commercialized or licensed to others.

The foreign filing decision should be made well before the expiry of the priority year (normally nine or ten months after the first filing date) to claim priority from the first application and allow translations, etc., to be prepared. Once the decisions have been made that a company should proceed with foreign filing and where it should file, the next consideration is how to proceed. One can either file nationally in each country where patent protection is required or, in the case of Europe, file regionally by filing a European patent application at the EPO designating up to thirty European states, or one can file via the Patent Cooperation Treaty (PCT), which allows a company to designate up to 125 nations. The PCT route enables a company to delay major costs up to twenty or thirty months after the first filing. Further, the PCT route gives a company more time when the commercial potential of an invention is not yet fully understood. Therefore, it is worthwhile to consider foreign filing via the PCT.

In case of imminent commercialization of the invention, it would appear appropriate to obtain patent protection quickly. In these circumstances, requests for accelerated examination of the patent application can be made before, for instance, the U.S., European, and Japanese Patent Offices. Alternatively, in Europe, it can be worth considering filing both a European patent application and national patent applications in important markets where one can get rapid grant, for example, in the Netherlands, France, Germany, and the United Kingdom. In addition to the filing of patent applications, the filing of utility models or the registration of design rights could be considered.

Patent Searches

If for reasons of urgency no patentability search was carried out prior to filing the first patent application, it is recommended to do so before deciding to file patent applications elsewhere. In this way, a company can avoid foreign filings for inventions that may not be patentable. In addition, in view of the search results the foreign filing text may need to be adjusted to enhance the chances of obtaining useful patent protection.

Series of Related Inventions

It is recommended to file patent applications on any trivial modifications disclosed in an important earlier patent application before the latter is published, which usually happens eighteen months after the first patent application is filed.

Ownership

It should be made sure that title to new inventions developed by a company's employees rests with the company. For taxation reasons, it is worth considering establishing an IP holding in a jurisdiction with a lower tax rate.

Enforcement Function

Patents can be powerful business tools; however, they are relatively expensive. Hence, it could be argued that a company should own only those patent rights it is prepared to defend. Indeed, defending a company's patent rights should in principle be central to an effective patent strategy.

To ensure that no third party infringes patents of a company, attention should be paid to the activities of its competitors. To that end, business and R&D personnel should watch closely publications and statements of competitors for any indications that they are or may be planning to work one or more of a company's patents. In addition, products of competitors could be analyzed.

Since patent litigation is very expensive, especially in the United States, and the outcome is never sure, the decision to start court proceedings is not an easy one. Nonetheless, there may be circumstances that clearly justify litigation against a competitor. The business and R&D functions should be completely briefed by the patent department on the possible pros and cons of such litigation action.

Infringement of Patents of Third Parties

General

A common misunderstanding is that having a patent means that one is free to use the invention oneself. However, it may well be the case that the patent covering a company's invention is dominated by a third party patent, and that by using its invention, the company would infringe the third party patent if it is valid and enforceable.

Infringement Studies

When a patent of a third party is potentially an obstacle to a company's present or future commercial operations, it is recommended to look into and address the matter immediately. If business and R&D personnel come across such patents, they should inform a patent professional about such a "problem patent" as early as possible.

However, it may well be that business and R&D personnel are not aware of any potential patent obstacles. It is therefore always recommended to carry out an infringement study (freedom to use study) in respect of new technologies/products that are of high commercial interest, especially since there is no obligation on the owner of a patent to grant licenses. This means that a patent professional needs to study the situation in close consultation with business and R&D personnel and that a legal opinion needs to be provided.

Infringement studies are, however, expensive and time-consuming exercises. It is therefore justified to conduct an infringement study only when it is clear that new technology will be commercially used. In addition, one should have a fairly proper understanding of the commercial operating conditions to enable a useful study to be carried out. It would be very expensive and time-consuming to perform infringement studies in respect of several technical options.

In respect of each country where the company expects to work the patent, a similar study may need to be carried out. However, it may well be that a potential infringement risk would exist only in certain countries while in other countries of the company's interest no patent filings took place.

It is good practice to obtain in respect of technologies/products of high commercial interest an opinion of noninfringement from an independent patent counsel, especially when the case is not clear-cut. This is of special importance in the United States because of possible triple damages claims.

Validity Studies

If there were to be an infringement problem, it is good practice to carry out a validity study in respect of the patent to see whether, in view of possible prior art, the patent can at least partly be considered to be invalid. If the patent is considered to be invalid, at least as far as the commercial operation of the business is concerned, it may be decided to ignore the patent, though the chance will exist that the patent owner may wish to take legal action. Therefore, before deciding to ignore a patent one needs to be pretty sure of the legal risk involved.

If the patent would appear to be valid and enforceable, the following options are available to a company:

* Ignore the patent, but this would be a business risk that needs to be avoided. In many countries infringement of a patent is considered a criminal offense. Further, willful infringement may result in the United States in triple damages claims.
* Try to engineer around the patent, thus avoiding infringement. By doing so it may well be that one makes a new invention that may be patentable and can force the owner of the other patent to negotiate a cross-license.
* Try to obtain a license to work under the patent in question.
* Try to acquire the patent or ultimately the company that owns the patent.

When a company tries to engineer around the patent this should result in an embodiment that is clearly outside the scope of the patent, not just an equivalent that only does not literally fall within the patent.

The reason for this is that in countries such as the United States, Germany, and Japan, the doctrine of equivalence applies, meaning that courts in these jurisdictions find that a patent is also infringed by a product or process that is not identical but merely similar (an equivalent) to the product or process explicitly described in the patent.

For this reason, engineering around another company's patent should be done in close consultation with patent professionals.

Monitoring Patent Activities of Third Parties

As mentioned earlier, an internal patents information database could possibly contain a section that would enable business and R&D personnel to identify third party patents that may constitute potential patent obstacles for a company's present or future commercial operations. Business and R&D personnel are advised to inform a patent professional as early as possible regarding such possible problem patents, thus ensuring that proper action can be taken at an early stage when needed.

Opposition Opportunities

Third party patents that would be an obstacle for a company's commercial operations could be opposed in, for instance, Europe, whereas in the United States reexamination proceedings are available. The following criteria could be considered for deciding whether to oppose a patent:

- Likelihood that a company's commercial operations or those of a licensee will infringe the claims of the patent
- Identification of new prior art that was not considered by the patent office in question
- Chances of knocking the patent out or limiting the scope of the claims in a way that is acceptable for the business are greater than 50 percent

Patent Assets Audits

If one wishes to manage the patent assets of a company in a proper manner, one needs to know at least what patent rights are owned by the company. A company's patent portfolio should therefore be evaluated on a case-by-case basis. In that way, deadwood can be pruned from the portfolio and unnecessary costs can be avoided. This is important since the maintenance of patent rights is relatively expensive in terms of renewal fees, which increase significantly in the course of a patent's lifetime. In addition, gaps in the patent portfolio could possibly be identified, as well as licensing opportunities. A patent asset audit should be conducted by patent professionals in close consultation with business and R&D personnel so as to obtain the business's views on the likely commercial significance of each invention, thus enabling informed decisions to be made.

It is further advisable to categorize the patent portfolio during the patent assets audit by linking each patent family to technologies and products and to indicate the commercial use and type of technology (e.g., breakthrough, incremental improvement, etc.) in respect of each patent family.

If it is no longer justified to maintain a patent right, the patent should be abandoned by nonpayment of the renewal fee, or in respect of the United States, a company could consider donating patent assets to a nonprofit organization to receive a tax relief. Alternatively, the patent assets could be sold to a third party. However, before one implements one of these options, it is advisable to consider the licensing potential of the patent assets in question.

During a patents assets audit it is also possible, though difficult, to ascribe an economic value to the patent assets of a business.

A survey of the patent portfolio could be made accessible to business and R&D personnel via, for instance, an internal patents information database.

Licensing

For many companies these days it is more attractive to license technology from others than to develop the technology themselves. An active approach to licensing technology to others could therefore prove to be a very attractive income source.

It may be useful to look into the possibility of licensing patented technology to others in areas that are no longer of interest to a company. However, an increasing number of companies are prepared to license their commercially important technology as well. To mine its patent portfolio properly and to find those inventions that others may want to license, a company should review its patent portfolio on a case-by-case basis.

Other companies working in the same technology area can be approached to see whether they may be interested in taking a license. Alternatively, from on-line databases it can be found out whether in the prosecution of another company's patent one of the company's patents has been cited. If so, it may well be that one of the company's patents would actually dominate the other company's patent, and the other company may be interested in taking a license from the company if it wishes to commercially work within the company's patent.

On the other hand, it may well be that a company wants to license patented technology from another company rather than developing technology itself. It should be kept in mind, however, that there is no obligation on the owner of a patent to grant licenses.

Due Diligence

To evaluate the patent assets of the other party in merger, acquisition, or joint venture negotiations, a patent due diligence needs to be carried out. In this way, an estimate of the value of the patent assets concerned can be obtained. In addition, embarrassing and costly surprises can possibly be avoided.

A proper patent due diligence contains at least the following elements:

- A listing of all the patent series in question
- Evidence to the effect that all the patent rights are owned by the other party
- In respect of each patent series, the legal status per country, including a statement whether any third party has filed an opposition or nullification action against the case concerned and an indication, where applicable, of a substantial limitation of the claims
- A statement of how the various patent series relate to commercial products/processes of the other party
- An estimate of the costs involved in the prosecution and maintenance of the patent series
- A statement of whether a freedom to use study has been carried out in respect of the commercial products/processes of the other party
- A statement of whether any third party has asserted that its rights are infringed by the commercial products/processes of the other party

- A statement of whether the other party has sent out any letters alleging infringement of its patent rights by others
- A statement of whether there are any licenses in existence, both where the other party licenses third parties under its patents or technologies and where the other party is licensing technology or patents from third parties
- Information concerning any joint research or development agreements of any type that have patent provisions in them

With respect to mergers, acquisitions, and joint ventures, it is recommended that business and R&D functions contact patent professionals for patent due diligence purposes as early as possible.

Oddball Inventions or Strategic Misfits

It may well be that during the R&D efforts of a company a new technology is developed that is of no interest to the company since its use is in a entirely different technology area. However, although the oddball invention or strategic misfit in question may be of no direct interest to a company, it may well be that it is of high potential interest to other companies operating in very different markets. Therefore, it may be useful to look into the possibility of offering the invention to others, either as a complete sales transfer or as a licensing opportunity. In that way, an additional flow of income could possibly be established from companies operating in different markets.

The Patent Strategy Document

When developing a patent strategy, patent professionals are recommended to discuss the above text in detail with senior managers of the business and R&D functions. In that way, informed decisions can be taken regarding the various available options and the recommendations that have been made in respect of each strategy element. Subsequently, the decisions in respect of each of these strategy elements need to be included in a patent strategy document.

Although a lengthy patent strategy document that includes a general discussion of each of the above elements will be useful for education purposes, it is unlikely that such a document will be very useful in the company's day-to-day operations. A "punchy" document highlighting only key points of the strategy is in practice more useful for business and R&D personnel. It is recommended to make both types of documents available to business and R&D personnel. Such a "punchy" document could read as follows:

General

Our patent strategy is designed to complement our business strategy. By means of this patent strategy the patent department intends to provide tailor-made and cost-effective support.

Patent Protection

We see the following three main reasons for seeking patent protection:

1) Exclusivity to obtain a competitive advantage
2) Licensing opportunities, i.e., to make money by licensing patent rights to others, but only in respect of noncore areas or nonstrategic activities when it makes commercial sense to do so, or to create cross-license opportunities
3) Use as a sales aid or marketing tool, for instance by marking products "Patent Pending," and for establishing credibility

Review of Inventions

We will carry out a patent search before drafting and filing a first application.

Filing Program

Inventions originating in the United States will be filed as U.S. provisional applications first. In respect of important inventions originating outside the United Sates, a U.S. provisional application will be filed at the same time as the first filing at the EPO.

We will make foreign filing decisions in line with standard foreign filing lists that reflect the strategic importance of the invention in question.

Enforcement Function

We consider defending our patent rights to be central to our patent strategy.

Infringement of Patents of Third Parties

Our business will respect, that is, not infringe, valid and enforceable patent rights of others, just as we expect others to respect our patent rights.

When we consider a patent of a third party to be a potential obstacle to our present or future commercial business operations, we will report the matter immediately to the patent department.

Infringement studies will be carried out in respect of new-to-market processes/products that are of high commercial interest, and in the United States we will obtain an opinion of noninfringement from an independent patent counsel.

Validity studies will be carried out if there are infringement problems, to see whether the patent can at least partly be considered to be invalid.

We will make decisions on whether to oppose third party patents on a case-by-case basis.

Patent Assets Audit

Once a year we will review our patent portfolio to ensure that deadwood is removed and unnecessary expenses thus avoided and to identify any possible gaps in our patent portfolio.

Due Diligence

With respect to mergers, acquisitions, and joint ventures, the business will contact the patent department for patent due diligence purposes as early as possible.

Review

When appropriate, this patent strategy will be changed/updated during our annual patent assets audit.

Conclusion

In this chapter, the elements have been discussed that form the foundation of a proper patent strategy. Every technology-based company should look into these elements. A company's patent strategy should ensure that the patent activities are tailored to its business needs. To establish this, a company's patent strategy needs to be aligned with the business and R&D objectives and strategies. In the next chapter, we learn how this can be achieved. There we learn to select the patent activities that are needed to realize true alignment of strategies. Subsequently, these selected patent activities need to be emphasized in the patent strategy. If the above thirteen elements form the foundation of a company's patent strategy, it will be through the company's committed efforts that the alignment of strategies will be built on that foundation.

Notes

1. Stephen C. Glazier, *Patent Strategy for Business* (Washington: LBI Law & Business, 1997); and H. Jackson Knight, *Patent Strategy for Researchers and Research Managers* (New York: John Wiley & Sons, Inc, 1996). These books are indeed essential reading. Actually, they awoke my interest in the field of patent asset management.

2. For an interesting discussion on advantages of provisional applications, reference is made to Philippe Signore, "The Benefits of Provisional Applications," *Managing Intellectual Property*, no. 114 (November 2001): 70-75.

3

Alignment of Strategies

The Concept of Strategy Alignment

In today's business world, the alignment of a company's patent, R&D, and business strategies is much sought after, but what does this really mean and how is this established in practice?

Central to the alignment of a company's strategies is the company's business vision, a statement that describes the company as it wishes to be in the future and defines the company's business objectives. The business vision will generally depend on matters such as company size, culture, competencies, and resources and constraints. A company needs to be committed to establishing its business objectives, and these objectives need to be challenging but realistic.

Once a business vision, and thus the desired future business position, has been defined, it is possible to define the R&D and patent positions that will support the desired future business position in the most effective manner. By doing so, one ends up with three ideal future positions, namely the desired business position, the desired R&D position, and the desired patent position. The plan of action aimed at realizing the desired future business position is the company's business strategy. Part of this plan of action is the company's efforts to establish the desired R&D position, enabling the company to develop or acquire the technologies that are needed to support the business objectives. The total of a company's R&D activities aimed at establishing the desired R&D position constitutes a company's R&D strategy. In turn, a patent strategy is the total of a company's efforts aimed at realizing the desired patent position and supporting the business and R&D objectives. The desired future positions and related strategies could be defined for the company as a whole or for each business area, technology area, or individual technology.

The alignment of the business, R&D, and patent strategies and the establishment of the business vision are schematically shown in figure 3.1.

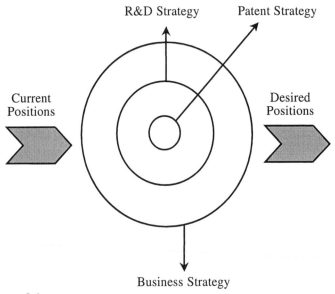

Figure 3.1
Establishing a Company's Business Vision

Understanding the Business Context

To ensure that a company's business, R&D, and patent strategies are aligned, it is essential that the R&D and IP functions understand the business context in which the company works. They should know the needs and objectives of the business and what it is that drives the business. In addition, the IP function should have a proper understanding of the company's R&D efforts and the company's R&D strategy. In turn, the business function (including the marketing and finance functions) should have an understanding of the abilities, capabilities, resources, and constraints of the R&D and IP functions. To make sure that the business and R&D functions have a basic understanding of intellectual property rights in general, and how these rights can be used as strategic business tools, an ongoing education effort should take place to improve intellectual property awareness within the company.

For the IP function to have a proper understanding of the company's business and R&D strategies, it needs to have access to all sorts of confidential information, including financial data and business strategy plans. In addition, the IP function needs to be seen as a key member of the business team to realize the company's future success. It is for these reasons that alignment of strategies and patent asset management needs to be managed top-down in a company. Experience teaches that the bottom-up management approach is not a valid option here for the simple reason that it would make alignment of strategies and patent asset management optional instead of a necessity within a company. A company must be strongly committed to establishing alignment of strategies, and its related activities should have full support of top management, including board members.

Further, before a company can decide where it wishes to go, it should first know where it presently stands. In other words, first the competitive landscape needs to be known. This means that the company's position in terms of market share, technology development, and patent activities must be assessed with respect to the competition. In that way, strengths, weaknesses, opportunities, and possible threats can be identified. In addition, factors such as market size and market growth and the relevance of technologies and patent rights in the marketplace need to be considered because they will make an IP function understand to what extent patent assets can be used as strategic business tools to realize the company's business goals. Since patents are relatively expensive to obtain and maintain, it is important to know whether the size and growth of the market justify patent protection. The cost of filing should always be weighed against the potential benefit of patent protection. Obviously, the larger the market, the easier it will be to recover the cost of filing. Also, the relevance of technology in the marketplace is an important factor to consider. In markets where technology plays an important, if not crucial, role, enabling companies to distinguish themselves from their competitors, the presence or absence of patent rights can make or break a company. It is not without reason that technology-driven markets show a high patent activity. On the other hand, in markets where technology plays only a relatively small role, the usefulness of patent protection could be doubtful. Further, to assess the usefulness of and need for patent rights in respect of a particular technology or product, one should know the role that patent rights play in the marketplace. Are patent rights aggressively enforced by competitors or are they mainly used for defensive purposes such as freedom of action?

Two Fundamental Requirements
for Effective Alignment

If one wants to establish alignment of strategies successfully there are two fundamental requirements that need to be met. First, an organizational structure should be put in place that ensures that informed business decisions could be made in respect of the company's patent assets. Second, the company should look at the task at hand from different angles that ideally complement each other. The latter can be done by looking into a number of areas of emphasis in respect of which a number of strategic options need to be considered and strategic recommendations need to be made. By doing so, a company will be able to select for each area of emphasis a set of particular patent activities that is aimed at accomplishing the alignment of strategies. Subsequently, these patent activities need to be emphasized in the patent strategy (see figure 3.2).

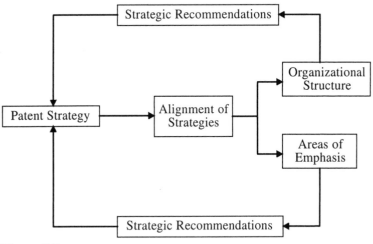

Figure 3.2
Effective Alignment of Strategies

The Organizational Structure

The organizational structure must make sure that the business, R&D, and IP functions contribute to the decision-making process at three different levels, namely a strategic and visionary level, projects level, and the day-by-day patent management level. To that end, at least the following multifunctional teams need to be in place:

- Strategy team
- Project teams
- IP management team

When required, a strategy team and IP management team need to be set up for each business area, each technology area, or each individual technology. Project teams will be put in place on an ad hoc basis.

Strategy Team

In the strategy team, the business, R&D, and patent strategies are developed in general terms, taking into account the current business environment and the available resources and possible constraints. These strategies should not be cast in concrete, and they need to be able to be adjusted whenever desired. In practice, this will usually mean that the strategies need to be reviewed at least once a year. Further, strategic recommendations will be considered and selected to establish alignment of strategies. This includes prioritization of projects and the allocation of resources. In addition, at this level, decisions will be made regarding licensing activities, enforcement, and patent dispute related issues, and advice will be given to top management regarding mergers, acquisitions, and divestments. Input from the IP function will include information about important IP trends as well as assessments of the company's patent position with respect to the competition. The strategic team should meet at least once a year, or whenever the need for a meeting arises. Obviously, senior managers should represent the business, R&D, and IP functions at this level.

Project Teams

A project team needs to be set up in respect of any strategic project that may have an impact on the company's future performance. Such projects will usually include major technology/product projects and matters such as mergers, acquisitions, and divestments. The project team should ensure that the project is aligned and stays aligned with the business strategy and that it is supported by R&D and IP activities. At this level, the IP function's activities include matters such as due diligence, competitive intelligence, and product clearance. Obviously, the project team should meet whenever required.

IP Management Team

In the IP management team the patent strategy is implemented and aligned with the R&D and business strategies on a day-to-day basis. At this level, decisions are being made regarding invention evaluation, prioritization of work, drafting and first filing, foreign filing, maintenance, oppositions, appeals, etc. The frequency of the IP management team's meetings will depend on the size of the company's patent portfolio and the volume of its related patent activities. The frequency of meetings should enable the team to perform its tasks in an adequate manner. It is good practice to have well-defined agendas covering the items to be discussed and to send related documents in advance to the participants, ensuring that decisions will be made in an efficient manner during the meetings.

It is recommended that project teams and the IP management team report to the strategy team, whereas the strategy team reports to

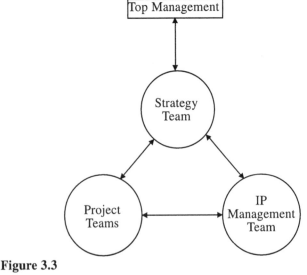

Figure 3.3
Organizational Structure

top management within the company. The organizational structure and the interaction between the teams is shown in figure 3.3.

The establishment of these teams may be considered self-evident, but how many IP professionals have not experienced being contacted for due diligence purposes at the last minute before a major acquisition was completed, leaving them no time to find any skeletons in the cupboard? How many companies have run into expensive patent disputes because no proper product clearance was carried out, and how many companies have developed and launched new and successful products only to lose their competitive edge quickly because of lack of adequate patent protection? Many companies, including multinationals with extensive patent portfolios.

Areas of Emphasis

When one wants to accomplish alignment of strategies, at least the following areas of emphasis need to be considered:

- Technologies necessary for future success
- Quality control
- Positions vis-à-vis the competition
- Cost control
- Sharing information across the company

By considering these areas of emphasis a company will be able to select a set of patent activities that will support the business and R&D goals in the best possible manner. As said before, these selected activities then need to be emphasized in the patent strategy. In that way, a company will realize true alignment of its patent strategy with its corporate goals.

Technologies Necessary for Future Success

When the business vision, and thus the desired business position, have been defined, the technologies can be identified that are necessary for the future success of the company. These technologies can generally be divided in three categories:

- Existing technologies available to the company

- Technologies under development that will become available to the company
- Missing technologies, which are technologies owned or being developed by others, that do not yet exist, or that are not yet under development

Once the necessary technologies have been identified, the R&D and patent activities need to be selected that will generate and protect these technologies in an effective manner or provide possible access to them in case the technologies are owned by someone else. In respect of each of these three categories, a number of R&D activities or options and patent activities can be considered, and these are discussed below. Obviously, those R&D and patent activities need to be selected that are best tailored to the company's needs.

Existing Technologies Available to the Company

- *R&D perspective:* No immediate actions may be needed. However, the company may wish to strengthen its current technology position by developing improvements over existing technologies or developing alternative embodiments.
- *Patent perspective:* At least the following patent activities need to be considered:
    - Check whether any gaps exist in the current patent portfolio, and if so, fill these gaps. In other words, make sure that the existing technologies are adequately covered by the company's patent portfolio.
    - Strengthen the patent portfolio. This could, for instance, be done by seeking protection for alternative embodiments and/or selection inventions that are not yet covered by the patent portfolio. A useful way to establish this is to organize invention-on-demand workshops (or patent factory sessions). In such workshops or sessions, inventors, in particular key inventors, are brought together with the aim to generate inventions in respect of a particular technology area.
    - Carry out a product clearance when the decision has been taken to commercialize a particular technology/product.
    - When a problem patent, that is, a patent that constitutes a potential obstacle to the company's future operations, has been identified, determine in consultation with the business

and R&D functions whether the problem patent can relatively easily be circumvented.

- In case the problem patent cannot easily be circumvented, determine to what extent the patent can be invalidated.
- When the patent can sufficiently be invalidated, approach the holder of the problem patent with the aim to obtain a royalty-free license to work the patent or, alternatively, ignore the patent and keep the arguments for invalidating the patent aside as ammunition until further notice.
- If needed, attack the problem patent. Depending on the jurisdiction in question, reexamination, opposition, or revocation procedures could be considered. This option should be given careful consideration since an unsuccessful attack may result in a weak position in possible subsequent licensing negotiations with the attacked third party.
- Identify patent rights in the portfolio and/or file patent applications that may hinder the owner of the problem patent in his own commercial operations. Such patent applications could cover selection inventions over the problem patent or alternative embodiments that are not covered by the problem patent itself. In that way, the owner of the problem patent may be forced to cross-license, thereby giving the company access to the desired technology.

Technologies Under Development That Will Become Available to the Company

- *R&D perspective:* One may wish to accelerate the development of these technologies by means of increased R&D efforts. Such efforts may include the development of alternative technologies and selection inventions. When only little progress in the development of the technologies has been made, it is worth considering acquiring technology from elsewhere or entering a joint development agreement with another company.
- *Patent perspective:* At least the following patent activities should be considered:
  - Ensure adequate patent protection in a timely manner. To establish this, an IP function may need to reshuffle its priorities and the drafting of patent applications may have to be outsourced.

- Make sure that ownership is established or clearly arranged in respect of outsourced R&D or joint developments.
- Check whether all patentable subject matter is already covered by the company's existing patent applications. Such subject matter includes alternative embodiments as well as selection inventions. If gaps exist, make sure these are filled. As said before, invention-on-demand workshops can be very effective for that purpose.
- Carry out patent searches to identify third party activity in the technical area concerned. Identify possible filing trends among competitors, and, if applicable, advise the business and R&D functions about potential problem patents and consider lines of action that may be required to deal with such patents.
- Look into ways of improving the company's patent position vis-à-vis particular competitors by penetrating their patent portfolios by filing patent applications that constitute selection inventions over their protected technologies or by surrounding competitors' patents by patent applications that cover alternative embodiments of the same technology or different applications of the same technology.
- Assist the R&D function in the identification of technologies and related patent rights that the company may wish to acquire from a third party.
- Undertake due diligence once the company has decided to acquire technologies and related patent rights from a third party.

Missing Technologies

- *R&D perspective:* When the required technologies are missing, various approaches are possible for a company, and the merits of each need to be considered carefully. The company may be able to develop the missing technology in-house. However, when this is not the case, the company may have to outsource the development of the technology to a third party that is in a better position to develop the technology concerned, or the company may wish to step into a joint development with a third party. Alternatively, the company could obtain access to the missing technology via cross-licensing or in-licensing, or the company could buy the missing technology and related patent rights outright from a third party. In case one needs to acquire or license the technology, it is, of course, important to obtain access to the technology at an early stage to ensure favorable financial terms.

- *Patent perspective:* At least the following patent activities should be considered:
    - Carry out patent searches to determine whether the missing technology has already been developed elsewhere and, if so, to what extent. Reinventing the wheel could thus possibly be avoided, and companies could be identified from whom one may want to license or acquire the technology or with whom one may wish to cooperate. Moreover, such search results may be used to give direction to the company's R&D efforts.
    - When the missing technology has already been developed or is currently under development by a third party, determine to what extent there is still room to create a technology and patent position for oneself. This may enable a company to create a bargaining position vis-à-vis the third party.
    - In case the missing technology and related patent rights are owned by a third party that is not prepared to give a license against acceptable financial terms, determine to what extent the patent right(s) can be invalidated and consider attacking the patent rights in question.
    - When the missing technology is owned by a third party, determine whether the company in turn owns technology and patent rights that could be of interest to the third party in question. In that way, the company may possibly obtain access to the missing technology by way of cross-licensing.
    - In case it is decided that the missing technology will be developed in-house, ensure that every technology developed is reviewed by the IP function in close consultation with the business and R&D functions and that adequate protection is sought at the earliest moment possible.
    - Ensure a high patent awareness among R&D personnel, especially key inventors, by means of invention-on-demand workshops and education programs. In that way, a company can ensure that opportunities within or outside the company are identified in a timely manner.

Quality Control

To ensure that the patent portfolio and related activities are tailored to the company's business needs, the quality of the patent portfolio should be checked periodically. In that way, strengths and weaknesses in the patent portfolio can be identified and, if required, appropriate action can be taken swiftly. Having an effective invention evaluation system in place is, of course, a first requirement to make sure that one has a patent portfolio of the right quality. But there is more to it. The following tools enable a company to check the quality of its patent portfolio and to identify possible strengths and weaknesses. When weaknesses or imbalances have been identified, the company may be required to redirect its R&D efforts; to educate business and R&D personnel on IP matters in areas that require improvement; to organize invention-on-demand workshops; and to adjust its foreign filing program. Further, the IP function may need to reshuffle its priorities to ensure that the most important things are done first. A company should go through these quality control processes regularly, at least once a year.

Strategic Importance versus Patent Volume

Do we have sufficient patent protection for the technology areas that matter most to the company? To find this out, one first needs to categorize the patent portfolio. This means that one has to link the patent assets to the various technology/product categories. By doing so, a number of subportfolios will be obtained that each relate to a particular technology/product area. A next step is to determine the strategic importance of each technology/product area or, if required, each technology/product. The strategic importance of a technology area will depend on various factors such as market size, market growth, market share, relevance of the technology in the marketplace, and type of technology involved. As to the latter, it will make, for instance, a difference when the technology concerned is a breakthrough or disruptive technology instead of a mature or basic technology. For these reasons, the strategic importance of technology areas needs to be determined in close consultation with the business and R&D functions. To be able to compare the strategic importance of the various technology areas with one another, one could use the following scale that runs from 1 to 5: 5 = very high strategic impor-

tance; 4 = high strategic importance; 3 = moderate strategic importance; 2 = low strategic importance; 1 = very low or no strategic
importance.

Subsequently, one determines to what extent patent coverage
exists for each technology area in terms of patent volume (number of
patent families), again using a scale ranging from 1 to 5: 5 = extensive
protection; 4 = substantial protection; 3 = moderate protection; 2 =
little protection; 1 = very little or no protection. Once the strategic
importance and the company's patent volume have been determined
for various technology areas they can be put in a matrix (see figure
3.4). From such an exercise it may, for instance, become clear that the
company's patent volume is large for a technology area X that is of
moderate strategic importance, whereas the patent coverage may be
little in respect of technology area Y that is of very high strategic
importance. Clearly such imbalance needs to be addressed, and
appropriate action should be undertaken to deal with the situation.

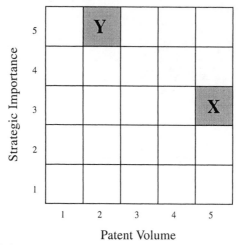

Figure 3.4
Strategic Importance versus Patent Volume

Strategic Importance versus Average Invention Value

Are our patents in highly important technology areas of sufficient
quality? To answer this question, the average quality of the inventions

should be compared with the strategic importance of the respective technology areas. Above, we saw how each technology area can be given a strategic importance value that ranges from 1 to 5. In the next chapter, we learn how to evaluate inventions, enabling us to distinguish important inventions from less important inventions by allocating to each invention a value that ranges from 1 to 5: 5 = high strategic importance; 4 = strategic importance; 3 = potential importance; 2 = limited potential importance; 1 = no importance. Once the entire patent portfolio has been properly evaluated on a case-by-case basis, it will be possible to determine the average invention value of each technology area. Subsequently, the average invention value can be compared with the strategic importance of the technology area in question (see figure 3.5). From figure 3.5 it could, for instance, become clear that the strongest inventions are being generated in technology area X that is of moderate strategic importance, whereas weak inventions are generated in technology area Y that is of very high strategic importance. Obviously, appropriate action is required to deal with such imbalance.

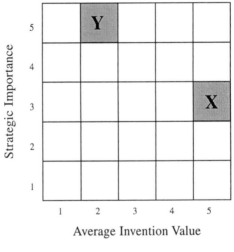

Figure 3.5
Strategic Importance versus Average Invention Value

Published with consent of Siemens AG/Dr. H. Goslowsky

Strategic Importance versus Portfolio Strength

What is the portfolio strength in respect of the technology areas that are of highest importance? This question can be answered by comparing the portfolio strength of the respective technology areas with the strategic importance of the technology areas. The strength of a company's patent portfolio will depend on the patent volume and the average quality (value) of its inventions and can be calculated by multiplying the former by the latter. Since, as we have seen above, both the patent volume value and average invention value range from 1 to 5, it follows that the value of the portfolio strength will range from 1 to 25. For the sake of ease, however, this range is brought back to a scale that also ranges from 1 to 5: 5 = portfolio strength of 21-25; 4 = portfolio strength of 16-20; 3 = portfolio strength of 11-15; 2 = portfolio strength of 6-10; 1 = portfolio strength of 1-5. In figure 3.6 the scores of the strategic importance and portfolio strength have been indicated for technology areas X and Y (see also figures 3.4 and 3.5). From figure 3.6 it can be concluded that the patent portfolio for technology area X is indeed much stronger than that for technology area Y, which in this case is most undesirable.

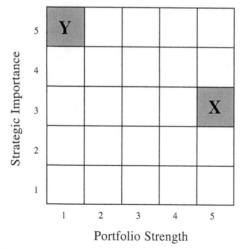

Figure 3.6
Strategic Importance versus Portfolio Strength

Global Coverage

Do we have adequate global coverage? To determine whether this is the case, one should check whether the patent portfolio or subportfolio (for each technology area) adequately covers the most important markets. This can be done by determining the extent to which patent protection is sought in the various countries (see figure 3.7). Moreover, the market size and expected growth in, for example, the next two years, the company's market share and desired growth over the same period of time, and the company's patent volume for various countries or regional markets can be compared (see figure 3.8). Figure 3.8 may provide a pointer that there is an imbalance between the patent volumes in Japan and China and that action may be needed to correct such imbalance.

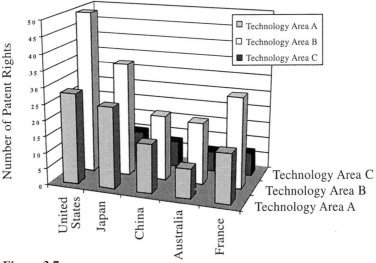

Figure 3.7
Global Coverage Per Technology Area

First Filing Trends

Are there any first filing trends that we should know about? By monitoring the number of first filings for each technology area over, for example, the last five years, possible trends may be identified (see

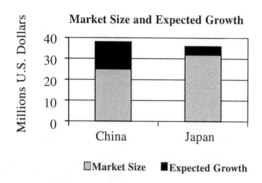

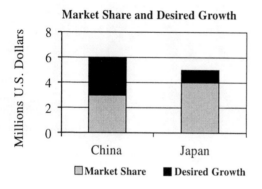

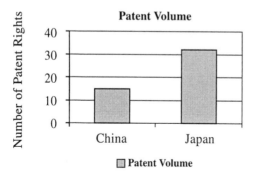

Figure 3.8
Global Coverage, Market Size, and Market Share

figure 3.9). For instance, when technology area A is of high strategic
importance and technology area B is of only limited strategic interest,
the filing trends identified require management to look into possible
causes for the declining number of first filings for technology area A.
Appropriate action could then be considered to reverse these trends.

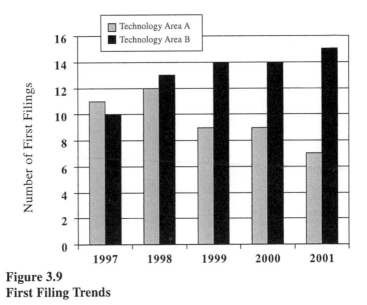

Figure 3.9
First Filing Trends

Legal Developments

Do we obtain the best legal protection possible? By keeping up to
date with legal developments in the various jurisdictions and anticipat-
ing important future developments, an IP function can influence the
quality of the patent portfolio considerably. In this respect, reference
can be made to developments such as second medical use claims and
the patentability of business methods and software as such in the
various countries.

Positions vis-à-vis the Competition

In today's global economy, companies are engaged in a survival
of the fittest contest. Their success, if indeed not their survival,

depends on how they strategically position themselves in the market-place. The next step in the alignment process is, therefore, to assess the company's current positions with respect to the competition and to see how they relate to the desired future positions as defined by the company's business vision. In that way, possible opportunities and threats can be identified. Obviously, opportunities need to be exploited, whereas threats need to be reduced. Opportunities arise when the company's current patent position is better than that of competitors. To improve the company's performance, the company could, for instance, exploit such a situation by out-licensing activities, by blocking others from the market, or by obtaining access to particular technologies of others by way of cross-licensing. On the other hand, when the company has a weak patent position vis-à-vis competitors, the company may become under threat because competitors may wish to exploit such a situation in a similar manner at the cost of the company. From the company's current positions immediate opportunities and threats can be identified. However, to obtain an understanding of possible future opportunities and threats, the company's desired future positions need to considered in the light of the current positions of competitors, their aggressiveness in the marketplace, and the trends in their filing programs.

The set of tools that is proposed in respect of this area of emphasis will enable a company to identify and anticipate possible opportunities and threats, and it will help a company to select those patent activities that assist the company in establishing the desired future positions.

However, before we can use these tools, the company's current positions need to be assessed. As far as the current business position is concerned, this needs to be done by the business function and is usually based on market share. The R&D function should determine the current R&D position, taking into account factors such as the maturity and breadth and depth of the technologies, whereas the assessment of the current patent position is the purview of the IP function.

Assessing the Patent Position

When one wants to obtain a proper understanding of the strength of a company's patent portfolio vis-à-vis competitors, both the quality and the size of the company's patent portfolio need to be compared with that of competitors. This is a difficult task, because many companies do not have a sufficient understanding of their own patent portfolios, let alone the portfolios of others. In addition, the size of patent portfolios is generally increasing, which makes such a task more difficult. Nonetheless, an effort should be made to obtain a proper understanding of the company's patent position because it is key to successful alignment of strategies.

Various methods are available to assess a company's patent position with respect to its competitors; their usefulness, however, can differ considerably.

Rule of Thumb

The least preferred method is the rule of thumb approach, which is based on the experiences of some individuals within the company from their dealings with competitors and does not involve any real investigation. Usually, this approach will result in a statement that the company has a leading position, middle position, or trailing position with respect to its main competitors. The outcome of this type of assessment can be wide of the mark.

Patent Volume

At the next level, the patent position is determined on the basis of a company's patent volume when compared to that of competitors. Patent volume is normally expressed as the total number of patent families or the total number of individual patent rights that has been published and that is owned by a company. This method is frequently used in markets where the various players have large patent portfolios. An evident drawback of this approach, however, is that it does not take any quality considerations into account. Having said this, a company might argue that it is fair to assume that the quality of its own inventions will roughly equal that of its main competitors. Although such an assumption may be correct, there is the danger that it is based on wishful thinking. Some companies are simply more innovative than others.

Patent Citation Index

In a yet more advanced method, the patent citation index is consi-

dered in addition to the company's patent volume to assess the
company's patent position. The patent citation index gives an indication of the average patent quality of a company compared to that of
others. It is based on the assumption that patents of high importance
are cited more frequently in subsequent patents and search reports
from patent offices than less important patents. The patent citation
index can be defined as the average number of citations received by
the company's patents that have been granted and published in a particular year, divided by the average number of citations received by all
patents granted and published in the same year and technology area.
When a company has a higher patent citation index than a particular
competitor, it is likely that the company's patents are more important
than those of the competitor. The strength of the company's patent
portfolio can then be defined as the number of the company's patent
rights multiplied by the patent citation index. By determining the
portfolio strength of the company and that of the main competitors the
company's patent position vis-à-vis these competitors can be assessed.
Some patent professionals are, however, skeptical about the usefulness
of the patent citation index, their arguments being that both applicants
of subsequent patents and patent examiners do not always cite the
most relevant prior art and that therefore the values of the patent
citation index will be "polluted." Although this may be true, it could
be argued that it is reasonable to assume that such "pollution" would
affect the various companies in a particular technology area to more
or less the same extent. Hence, and despite some skepticism, it may be
useful to compare the company's patent citation index with those of
competitors to assess the company's patent position. Further information about the patent citation index can be found on the web site of
CHI Research, a company that has developed databases to determine
patent citation indices.

Case-by-Case Basis

Finally, one could evaluate the portfolios of competitors on a
case-by-case basis, using the same evaluation criteria that the
company uses to evaluate its own cases. However, it will be clear that
this is not a valid option in respect of very large patent portfolios. In
that case, one could decide to evaluate only relatively small and
comparable samples of cases from the company's portfolio and those
of competitors. Alternatively, one could decide to limit patent

mapping exercises to the technology areas that are of the highest
strategic importance, to focus on a particular competitor only, to
consider only those patent assets that have been filed during the last
five years, or a combination of these possibilities.

Strategic Importance versus Patent Position

Do we have strong patent positions vis-à-vis the competition in
respect of the technology areas that matter most to the company? To
find this out, the strategic importance of technology areas could be
compared with the company's related patent positions, and the results
can be put in a matrix as shown in figure 3.10. In figure 3.10, the value
of the patent position ranges from 1 to 5: 5 = leader; 4 = major player;
3 = moderate player; 2 = small player; 1 = very small or no player.
From figure 3.10 it is clear that the company's patent position is strong
in respect of technology area A that is of moderate strategic importance, whereas the patent position is weaker in respect of technology
area B that is of very high strategic importance. It will be clear that
such imbalance needs to be addressed. Further, figure 3.11 is of
interest since it may enable a company to identify licensing, merger,
acquisition, and divestment opportunities, depending on the patent
position of the company with respect to competitors and the strategic
importance of the technology area in question. For instance, competitor A might be interested in licensing patents and technology from the
company in respect of technology areas A and E. Figure 3.12 gives a
more detailed picture of the patent positions of the company and
competitors C and D in respect of a particular technology. The understanding that competitor C has many patents but of a relatively low
quality can have a major impact on licensing negotiations with this
competitor.

Global Coverage

Do we have sufficient global coverage when compared with
competitors? To answer this question the company's foreign filing
program could be compared with those of the main competitors. Such
an exercise may trigger interesting questions. For example, why do we
file fewer patent applications in particular countries than one or more
of our competitors (see figure 3.13)? Such information is particularly
interesting when combined with information about market size and

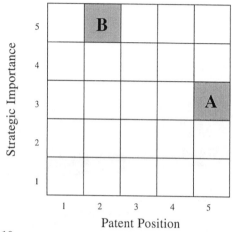

Figure 3.10
Strategic Importance versus Patent Position

Published with consent of Siemens AG/Dr. H. Goslowsky

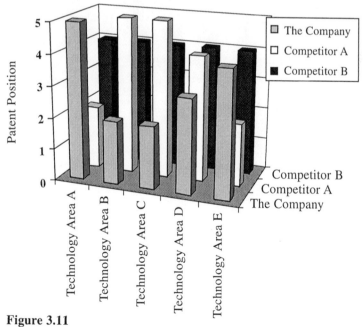

Figure 3.11
Patent Positions of Technology Areas vis-à-vis Competitors

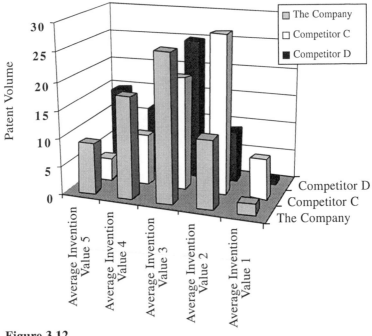

Figure 3.12
Detailed Patent Position vis-à-vis Competitors

market share (see figure 3.14). Figure 3.14 may, for instance, tell us
that competitor B has a foreign filing program that does not make
sense in respect of China. On the other hand, it may be a sign that
competitor B intends to use its patents against others in China in the
foreseeable future to increase its market share at the expense of others.

Filing Trends

   Are there any filing trends among competitors that we should
know of? By comparing the company's filing pattern with the filing
patterns of main competitors, possible trends and potential areas of
risk could be identified. It should be recognized, however, that even
the most recently published patent application was first applied for
eighteen months ago and is likely based on work done two to two and
a half years ago. In figure 3.15 the numbers of new publications
(eighteen months after the first filing date) are shown for the company

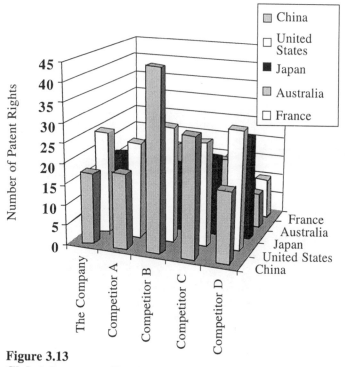

Figure 3.13
Global Coverage—Foreign Filing

and some competitors for a particular technology area and period of time. From figure 3.15 it is clear that competitors C and D are filing an increasing number of patent applications in this particular area, whereas the company itself remains at about the same filing level. Do competitors C and D know something important we don't know about or are they just wasting on purpose a lot of money? These are important questions, especially because an increasing number of companies, including one's own immediate competitors, are making efforts to improve the cost-effectiveness of their patent portfolios. Hence, it is not likely that they are willingly wasting resources. These questions become even more important if the technology area in question is considered of only relatively low strategic importance to the company. Could it be that the company has an incorrect perception regarding the strategic importance of this particular technology area? This surely needs to be checked with the business and R&D functions,

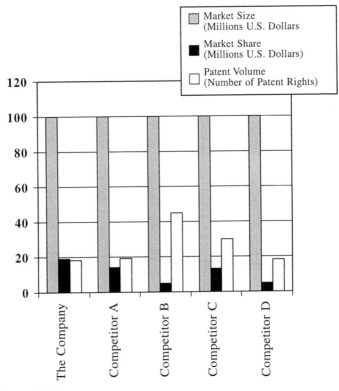

Figure 3.14
Market Size, Market Share, and Patent Volume in China

because it may turn out that the company is heading in the wrong direction.

Patent Position versus Business Position

Once the business and patent positions have been assessed, these positions can be compared with each other. A matrix like the one shown in figure 3.16 enables a company to identify possible imbalances and triggers important questions that need to be answered. Moreover, it requires a company to consider various strategic options when imbalances are identified. In figure 3.16, the respective positions of two technology areas X and Y are shown. Both the business and patent positions have been given scores that range from

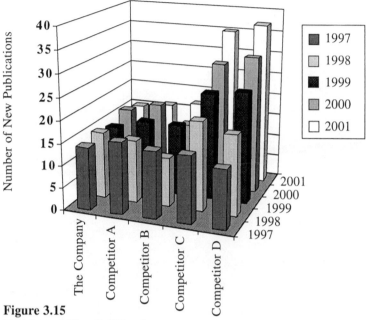

Figure 3.15
Number of New Publications

1 to 5: 5 = leader; 4 = major player; 3 = moderate player; 2 = small player; 1 = very small or no player.

Technology Area X—Strong Patent Position versus
Weak Business Position

As regards technology area X, the company's patent position appears to be clearly stronger than its related business position. Is this in line with the company's strategies, or is the company's investment in patents too high for technology area X? The investment in patents may indeed be too high when technology and patents play only a minor role of importance in the marketplace. In that case, the company should consider abandoning or donating (in the United States) patent assets that are no longer of real interest to the company. In addition, one may wish to adjust the company's foreign filing program and to be more selective in respect of its first filings. On the other hand, it could well be that it is the company's corporate goal to

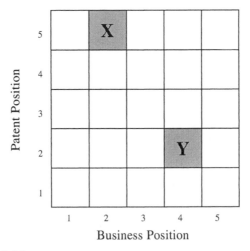

Figure 3.16
Patent Position versus Business Position

Published with consent of Siemens AG/Dr. H. Goslowsky

become the market leader in this technology area in a few years time
and that the strong patent position could be used to establish this goal,
for instance, by enforcing the company's patent rights and generating
a licensing income.

Technology Area Y—Weak Patent Position versus
Strong Business Position

   Regarding technology area Y we have quite the opposite situation.
Here the company's business position is much better than its related
patent position. This situation may be justified when the relevance of
technologies and patent rights is relatively low in the marketplace.
However, when technology and patent rights play an important role in
the marketplace, it may be that the company's investment in patents is
(much) too low and that the company may lose market share to a
competitor that intends to use its stronger patent portfolio against the
company at some stage in the future. When the investment in patents
is too low, the company should consider increasing quickly the
strength of its patent portfolio. In addition to invention-on-demand
workshops to generate high-quality inventions, one could consider a

joint development with another company, or one could consider acquiring patent assets from a third party. Further, one could consider adjusting the company's foreign filing program, and being less selective regarding its first filings. However, as to the latter option, one should realize that although the company's patent volume will increase, the quality of the patent portfolio is likely to be affected.

Patent Position versus R&D Position

In a similar manner, the company's patent position can be compared with its R&D position. In figure 3.17 the positions of four different technology areas A, B, C and D are shown. The value of the R&D position ranges from 1 to 5, using a similar scale as the one used for the business and patent positions. Also figure 3.17 enables a company to identify possible imbalances. It triggers the right kind of questions and enables a company to consider the various strategic options.

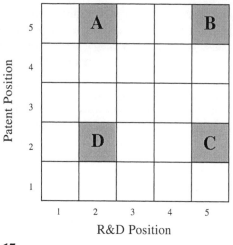

Figure 3.17
Patent Position versus R&D Position

Published with consent of Siemens AG/Dr. H. Goslowsky

Technology Area A—Strong Patent Position versus
Weak R&D Position

Clearly, the company's patent position is much stronger than its
R&D position. Is this justified or is the company's investment in
patents too high? In this respect, it should first be realized that it is in
general unlikely that a small technology player will be a patent leader.
However, it may be that it is the company's corporate goal to become
the technology leader in this technology area in order to realize its
business goals. The strong patent position could then, for instance, be
used to assist the company in obtaining access to third party technologies via cross-licensing, or the company's revenues, and thus its
R&D budget, can be increased by out-licensing activities.
Alternatively, the company may wish to look into a joint development
or merger with another company, or it may decide to divest this part
of the business.

Technology Area B—Strong Patent Position versus
Strong R&D Position

In this situation, a company could well decide to use its patents
mainly for offensive purposes. The company may consider enforcing
its patent rights to improve the company's business position in the
marketplace. In respect of the enforcement option, two aspects need to
be considered before any action is initiated. First, the market size and
market growth need to be checked. It may well be that the market is
simply too big to be covered by the company alone. In that case, out-
licensing could be a better option. Second, it must be checked within
the company whether an enforcement action could possibly backfire
one way or the other. In addition, when the company has both a strong
patent and a strong technology position, the company has an attractive
platform to start out-licensing activities in an active manner. Further,
the company could possibly enter a cross-license agreement to
establish freedom of action, whereby the other party would be
prepared to pay the company a royalty because of the company's
superior technology and patent positions.

Technology Area C—Weak Patent Position versus Strong R&D Position

The company's R&D position is stronger than the patent position. Does this mean that the company's technologies are insufficiently protected by the company's patent portfolio, or do the company's technologies mainly constitute know-how that the company does not wish to patent? In case of the former, the company should increase its patenting efforts to improve the patent position vis-à-vis competitors, provided that technology and patents are of relevance in the market-place. This may be established by invention-on-demand workshops, adjustment of a company's foreign filing program, and by being less selective at the first filing stage, though the latter option needs careful consideration. In addition, the company may need to improve it processes/procedures. For instance, it may need to decrease the time from invention report to first filing, or alternatively, it may need to outsource drafting work to outside agents. Another option could be to acquire patent assets from a third party. In case most of the company's technologies would constitute know-how, the company could consider analyzing the patent landscape for the technology area concerned. It may well be their restrained attitude toward patenting is fully justified in the light of the role that patents play in this field of business. On the other hand, such analysis may reveal that competitors have already patented the same type of know-how, and that this may become a threat to the company.

Technology Area D—Weak Patent Position versus Weak R&D Position

Does a situation like this mean that the company will have great difficulty surviving in the future? Not necessarily. When patents and technology play only a minor role in the market, and the company's success really depends on its marketing skills rather that its technologies, this situation may be acceptable. Having said this, it should, of course, be noted that within most industries the dependence on new technologies is rapidly increasing, and this trend is unlikely to be reversed in the foreseeable future. Hence, the situation in respect of technology area D will likely be bad news for a technology-based company. In a situation like this, of course, an attempt should be made to strengthen the patent position by way of the various options mentioned earlier in respect of technology area C. However, in this situation, expectations as to the effectiveness of invention-on-demand workshops should be tempered, especially when the technology gap with respect to immediate competitors is very big. In addition, mergers or joint developments could be considered with third parties that have technology and patent portfolios that would complement that of the company, or the technology and patent assets could be acquired from another company. Last, the company could consider to divest this part of their business. Whichever of these options will be selected, the company should consider to conduct product clearances in respect of products that are of high commercial relevance, especially when technology and patents are important within the marketplace. In case potential problem patents are identified, one should consider to attack such patents, keeping in mind that such action, if not successful, may badly backfire in subsequent licensing negotiations.

Gaps Analysis

Although the above tools are as such already helpful, it should be realized that they essentially focus on the company's current positions only. They give us an incomplete picture, because they tell us where we are, but not where we wish to go. What one really needs to do is to look into both the company's current positions and its desired future positions and, then, to select those patent activities that will help to close any possible gap between the company's current positions and the desired future positions.

For the sake of ease, it is assumed that a technology-based company will choose a business vision and corresponding desired future positions that in general terms resemble one of the simplified business visions and desired future positions that have been set out in figure 3.18. A business vision can be developed for each business area, technology area, or, if required, individual technology.

Although the business vision and the desired future positions will often be in one and the same row in figure 3.18, this is not necessarily the case. It could, for instance, be that a company wants to exit a parti- cular market, thereby relinquishing its business and R&D positions, while it may need or wish to maintain its patent position, at least for the time being, for out-licensing purposes. On the other hand, a company may wish to obtain strong business and R&D positions, while it may not be interested in obtaining a strong patent position

	Desired Positions			Current Positions		
Business Vision	Business Position	R&D Position	Patent Position	Business Position	R&D Position	Patent Position
To become or remain the market leader	**Market leader**	**Technology leader**	**Patent leader**	Market leader	Technology leader	**Patent leader**
To become or remain a major player	Major player	Major player	Major player	**Major player**	**Major player**	Major player
To become or remain a moderate player	Moderate player	Moderate player	Moderate player	Moderate player	Moderate player	Moderate player
To become or remain a small player	Small player	Small player	Small player	Small player	Small player	Small player
To become or remain a very small or no player	Very small or no player	Very small or no player	Very small or no player	Very small or no player	Very small or no player	Very small or no player

Figure 3.18   Current Positions and Desired Positions

because patent rights may play only a relatively small role in the marketplace concerned.

When a business vision and its desired business, R&D, and patent positions have been defined, the current business, R&D, and patent positions need to be determined and analyzed with respect to the competition. Subsequently, the current positions should be compared with the desired future positions and possible gaps between the various positions need to be identified. The next step is to develop strategies for filling or closing the gaps that have been identified, thus ensuring that the desired business, R&D, and patent positions will be realized.

It is important to consider both the desired positions and current positions, as is shown in figure 3.18, where both the desired and current positions have been indicated for a particular technology. When only the current positions would be considered, one could possibly conclude that the company in question would invest an unjustifiably high amount of money in patents, and that consequently the volume of patent work would need to be reduced. However, when the company's business vision and corresponding desired future positions are also taken into account, it becomes clear that the volume of patent work actually needs to be maintained or may even need to be increased to improve the business and R&D positions, for instance, by out-licensing and cross-licensing activities.

Strategic Recommendations for Filling the Gaps

A variety of gaps can exist between the respective current and desired positions. For instance, a company may wish to become the technology leader in a particular technology area, but currently it may not be more than a moderate player from a technology perspective. Moreover, gaps may exist between the current business, R&D, and patent positions. For example, a company can be a moderate player from a patent perspective, whereas at the same time it can be a technology leader.

Here, we will discuss only the gaps in respect of which an IP function can take immediate action. In this respect, there is an important point to make, which is that the activities of an IP function will obviously have a direct impact on the patent position, whereas these activities will usually not directly influence the business or technology position of the company. To give an example, in the pharmaceutical industry, where patent protection is essential for doing business, the impact of patents is often only fully recognized about ten years after the patent applications have been filed, because it normally takes such a long time to take a new product to market. On the other hand, the activities of an IP function may, of course, indirectly steer the business and technology positions in a desired direction. This could, for instance, be established by the generation of a licensing income that adds directly to the bottom line, part of which subsequently may be invested in the company's R&D efforts. Equally, the company's patent activities may provide the company access to desired/missing third party technology by way of cross-licensing. It will be appreciated that such impacts will become apparent only in the course of time, for they are not established overnight. Another point to make is that the strength of the company's patent position will obviously depend on the success of its R&D efforts. A weak technology position usually does not go hand in hand with a strong patent position.

It is believed that the following possible gaps are of interest to an IP function because it can take immediate action to fill or close them:

- The current patent position is weaker than the desired patent position.
- The current patent position is stronger than the desired patent position.
- The current patent position is stronger than the current R&D position, and the latter is weaker than the desired R&D position.
- The current patent position is stronger than the current business position, and the latter is weaker than the desired business position.

In respect of each of these gaps a number of patent activities should be considered, and those activities must be selected that assist the company in closing the gap in question.

The Current Patent Position Is Weaker Than the Desired Patent Position

Various reasons may apply why the current patent position would be too weak. For instance, the company may just have entered a business field that is new to it; the company may be a start-up company; the company may have neglected its patent portfolio; or the relevance of patents has suddenly become more important in a market where patents traditionally played a minor role, because a particular competitor has changed the "patent game" by starting to file a lot of patent applications and enforcing its patents aggressively against competitors.

When the company's current patent position needs to be strengthened, at least the following patent activities should be considered:

- Increase the size of the patent portfolio and improve its quality. This can be realized by means of invention-on-demand workshops. This could be particularly effective when the R&D position is strong but the patent position is weak and is especially important to technology areas that are of high strategic importance. The extent to which global coverage is sought also needs to be considered, especially in view of increasingly aggressive and truly global competition. This may mean that the company's foreign filing program may need to be adjusted.

- Make sure business and R&D personnel have a basic understanding of patents and IP in general. As such, patent awareness within the company will improve, and personnel may become more active in reporting new ideas/technical developments.

- Improve internal and external processes/procedures. One could think of trying to shorten the time to review reported inventions. In addition, one could look into the possibility of speeding up examination proceedings, by requesting accelerated examination or selecting less time-consuming filing routes, for example, national filings instead of the PCT route. This option is particularly important when the R&D position is strong but the patent position is weak.

- Acquire patent rights of others. Third party patents could be identified that would complement or fit into the company's patent portfolio and that a third party is willing to sell. Clearly, this option requires an active approach and absence of the "not invented here" syndrome.

- Conduct product clearances for products of relatively high commercial relevance and of which one has a proper understanding of the commercial operating conditions. This is especially important when both the patent and R&D positions are weak and patents play an important role in the marketplace.

• Attack dominating patents of others that are not subject to current (cross) licensing agreements. This option is particularly important when both the patent and technology positions are weak. However, as said before, one should make sure that such action does not backfire in the sense that it would deteriorate one's negotiation position vis-à-vis the attacked patent holder at a later stage.

The Current Patent Position Is Stronger Than the
Desired Patent Position

Although patent assets are becoming increasingly important business tools, it could nonetheless happen that a company's current patent position is stronger than the desired one. One could think of various reasons why such a situation could arise. The main reason will be that the company's patent portfolio and related patent strategy are not aligned with the company's business objectives. The trouble with patent assets is, as some put it, that once filed, a patent application starts to have a life of its own, and there is nothing to stop it. Once the first filing and foreign filing costs have been incurred, one may become hesitant to abandon a case. Often it is thought that the case should be at least of some value, because otherwise the case would not have been filed in the first place, and so the case lives on. In addition, many decision makers do not want to run the risk of killing a case that later becomes of commercial interest, though the likelihood that this may happen is small. While such a situation may have been quite common in the past, today's business environment dictates a different approach to a company's filing and maintenance policies. Patent assets are relatively expensive, and if they do not provide a competitive advantage, such assets should simply not be pursued.

A possible other reason why the current patent position is stronger than the desired one could be that the technologies covered by the patent portfolio have been superseded. Also, the company may have decided to exit a particular market.

When the current patent position is stronger than desired, each case should be judged on its own merits, taking into account the strategic purposes of the patent portfolio. Does the company mainly want to establish freedom of design, or is it also interested in licensing its patent assets actively to others, including immediate competitors and companies that are operating in entirely different markets? In the former case, one may wish to prune dead wood from the existing patent portfolio in a somewhat rigorous manner, for instance, by setting a tight target for the number of cases that need to be abandoned. In the latter case, however, one may wish to maintain a much higher volume of cases for out-licensing purposes.

When the current patent position is stronger than required, at least the following patent activities should be considered:

- Out-license and/or cross-license to generate royalty income. In that way, the business position could be improved since such an income stream will have a direct impact on the company's bottom line. A company may wish to limit itself to out-licensing its noncore technology. However, an increasing number of companies are prepared to out-license their core technologies as well.
- Cross-license to obtain access to technologies in other technology areas. For instance, company A may have a strong patent position in technology area X in which it no longer has interest. Company B, however, is interested in technology area X and may wish to obtain a license. In turn, company A may be interested to obtain access to technology area Y in which company B has a strong patent position. In such a situation, company B could be interested in cross-licensing with company A.
- Be more selective at the first filing and foreign filing stages, in the sense that only cases that really matter to the company are filed. In relation to this, the company's evaluation criteria for its inventions and its foreign filing program may need to be adjusted.
- Sell patent rights outright to third parties, or consider IP donations in the United States. This is especially of interest in respect of noncore technology areas.
- Abandon patent series that are no longer of interest or only of limited interest, partly or completely, taking into account possible interest of other business units within the company.

The Current Patent Position Is Stronger Than the
Current R&D Position, Whereby the Latter Is Weaker
Than the Desired R&D Position

In a situation like this, at least the following patent activities could be considered:

- Improve the company's R&D position by obtaining access to third party technology by way of cross-licensing
- Generate revenues by licensing activities to allow a company to increase its R&D budget

*The Current Patent Position Is Stronger Than the
Current Business Position, Whereby the Latter Is Weaker
Than the Desired Business Position*

In this situation, the patent position can be used to improve the business position. Patent activities that need to be considered include:

- Block competitors from the market by enforcing the company's patents, thus enabling the company to increase its market share
- Out-license and/or cross-license to third parties to generate licensing revenues
- Attack third party patents that may constitute potential obstacles for the company's commercial operations, with the purpose to remove the patent completely or to establish a limitation of the claims that is acceptable for the company's commercial operations

In respect of each of the described gaps, those patent activities should be selected that are believed to close the gap in the most efficient and cost-effective manner, whereby it must be realized that this is not likely to happen overnight, but that this may take a substantial effort over a period of time. The choice of patent activities will obviously depend on the size of the gap between the current patent position and the desired patent position and the time and effort that are likely required to fill the gap.

Exposure Analysis

To assist in the identification of possible opportunities and threats, a relatively simple analysis can be used in addition to the above tools. In this analysis a company's potential exposure to threats of competitors can be determined, and vice versa. The exposure of a company to a particular competitor can be defined as the total sales of the company in respect of the technology area in question multiplied by the portfolio strength (number of patent families x average invention value) of the competitor, whereas the exposure of this parti-

cular competitor to the company can be defined as the total sales of
the competitor multiplied by the portfolio strength of the company.
When these exposures are about the same, there is a balance between
the positions of the company and the competitor. On the other hand,
when the exposure of the company to the competitor is smaller than
that of the competitor to the company, the company is in a favorable
position with respect to the competitor, and an opportunity may exist
vis-à-vis the competitor in question, for example, licensing opportunities. Conversely, when the exposure of the company to the competitor
is greater than that of the competitor to the company, the company is
in an unfavorable position with respect to the competitor, and the
company may be exposed to a possible threat since the competitor
may intend to offensively use its patents against the company at some
later time. To give an example, let's assume that company A's total
sales amount to $200 million U.S. and that its patent portfolio strength
has a value of 600 (200 patent families x average invention value of
3), whereas competitor B's total sales amount to $250 million U.S.
and its patent portfolio strength equals 300 (100 patent families x
average invention value of 3). Using the exposure analysis this would
mean that company A's exposure equals 200 multiplied by 300,
whereas competitor B's exposure to a threat amounts to 250 multiplied by 600. Hence, from this analysis it could be concluded that
competitor B would potentially be exposed to company A, which in
the light of the figures may be a realistic conclusion, provided that
patents and technology play an important role in the marketplace. In
fact, taking a step back, the usefulness of this entire exercise is based
on the assumption that patents and technology are equally important
to competitors. In addition, one should have a realistic view on the
patent portfolio strength of both the company itself and competitors.
Having more patent rights than another, and about the same total sales,
does not necessarily mean that there would exist an opportunity vis-à-
vis a competitor. First, patents may play only a relatively small role in
the marketplace, justifying only a limited patent activity. Second, the
average quality of one's large patent portfolio may be questionable.

The exposure analysis is straightforward when the average
invention values of both the company and competitor are known.
However, this may not always be the case, especially when the portfolios in question are very large. In that case, one may wish to
consider in this analysis patent volumes instead of portfolio strengths,
assuming an equal average invention value for both the company and

the competitor. As said earlier, this may be misleading because some companies are simply more innovative than others. Alternatively, one could evaluate relatively small samples of competitors' portfolios and extrapolate the results to their whole portfolios.

To exploit opportunities or to reduce threats that have been identified by means of the exposure analysis, the company could at least consider the following patent activities:

Opportunities

- Out-licensing and/or cross-licensing. Competitors that are highly exposed to the company could be contacted to exploit licensing opportunities. They may be persuaded or forced to enter a license agreement.

Threats

- Strengthen the patent portfolio. Competitors may have been identified that may wish to use their stronger patent portfolio against the company. In that case, a company should consider improving its patent portfolio rapidly. As we have seen before, this could, for instance, be realized by invention-on-demand workshops, increased filing efforts, and improved internal procedures. In addition, a company could improve the patent coverage in respect of particular markets where competitors have stronger positions. To that end, foreign filing programs may need to be adjusted and alternative filing routes may need to be considered, such as the filing of provisional U.S. applications.
- Cross-licensing. The company may feel exposed to a particular competitor, and a cross-license from the competitor may be necessary to establish freedom of action.

Aggressiveness of Competitors

Competitor aggressiveness is directly related to competitor threat. This means that the aggressiveness of competitors, and thus likelihood of patent disputes, should be assessed to obtain a proper understanding of possible threats. Such assessment can be based on the company's knowledge and experience, various news sources (e.g., the Internet), and legal dispute databases such as Litalert.

Cost Control

Since patents are relatively expensive to obtain and maintain, it is important that these assets are cost-effectively managed. In view of profit margins that are increasingly under pressure this has become of greater importance than ever before. A company that wishes to manage its patent assets in a cost-effective way should at least look into the following items:

IP Holding

Establishing an IP holding in a jurisdiction with a lower tax rate can provide substantial fiscal advantages. The underlying idea is that the IP holding owns the company's intellectual property and that it allows the company's associated businesses to use the intellectual property by means of internal licenses. In turn, the associated businesses pay royalties to the IP holding.

IP Donations

In the United States it is possible to donate intellectual property to a nonprofit organization and to receive in turn a tax relief. An increasing number of companies are using this option to remove nonstrategic patent assets from their patent portfolios and to receive in return financial benefits. However, the procedures are not simple and can be time consuming. The intellectual property needs to be properly valued, and the valuation needs to be accepted by the U.S. tax authorities.

Costs to Date/Cost Forecasts

Cost control obviously includes an understanding of the patent costs to date and the costs that will arise in the foreseeable future. Such information is important since it can assist a company in obtaining insights in the return on investment regarding its patent assets. Moreover, it will assist businesses in preparing their patent budgets. This information could be made available to the business and R&D functions by means of an internal patent information database.

IP Insurance

Patent litigation is very expensive, especially in the United States. Various insurance companies provide patent insurance packages that are aimed at minimizing a company's financial exposure in case of patent litigation, both from infringement and enforcement perspectives.

Use and Choice of Outside Agents

A company should make sure that it uses high-quality outside agents that charge competitive fees. Fees among local agents can differ substantially, and it is therefore good practice to check whether the fees of the agent of the company's choice are acceptable and not clearly out of line with the market. In addition, it will be beneficial to concentrate the work in each country with only a few outside agents. In that way, discounts can be negotiated.

Outsource Out-Licensing

Successful out-licensing requires a committed effort and a substantial investment to start with. Successes will not come overnight. Actually, it usually takes at least a few years before real results are achieved. A possible option therefore is to use a consultancy firm that will do the out-licensing job for you on a commission basis.

Improve Processes and Procedures

Looking into the cost-effectiveness and efficiency of an IP function's processes and procedures should be an ongoing process. One should continuously try to avoid duplication of work by more effective delegation. Further, the most cost-effective filing routes should be used while ensuring that the business objectives will be met, and possibilities such as electronic report of inventions and the direct electronic filing of patent applications at patent offices should be considered.

Sharing Information across the Company

When for a particular business or technology area, a strategy
team, project teams, and an IP management team have been put in
place to facilitate alignment of strategies, information will be shared
across the business or technology area in question. However, the
sharing of information across a company needs to be brought to a
higher level when the company consists of a number of separate
business units that are engaged in related technologies. In that case,
areas of mutual interest arise that require close attention to ensure that
decisions will be made in the best interest of the company.
Independent of whether the patent assets are centrally owned and
managed or separately controlled by each business unit, all parties that
have a potential interest in a particular patent asset should provide
input to the decision-making process. Such stages include the
invention review stage and the foreign filing and maintenance stages.
In addition, their input is required in respect of licensing decisions and
enforcement actions against third parties. In that way, a company
could possibly avoid shooting itself in the foot. A particular business
unit may, for instance, wish to initiate court proceedings against a
third party because it infringes one of the company's patents.
However, at the same time, another business unit may wish to start a
joined development with the same third party and may want to avoid
a legal dispute at all cost. It is for reasons like this that patent information should be shared across a company. To that end, a framework
should be put in place that automatically requires potentially interested parties to provide input to the decision-making process. This could
be realized by way of an internal patents information database.

Conclusion

In this chapter we have learned that there are two fundamental requirements to be met when a company wants to establish alignment of
strategies in an effective manner. An organizational structure needs to
be in place that ensures that the various functions contribute to the
decision-making process at different levels, and the company needs to
look into a number of particular areas of emphasis to make sure that
the task at hand is looked at from different angles that complement

each other. In respect of these areas of emphasis, tools were discussed that enable a company to consider and select those patent activities that are required to realize true alignment of strategies. Together these tools may require a company to consider a particular patent activity more than once. This is unavoidable and is as such no problem, because it is better to reconsider an option than not to have considered the option at all. Alternatively, one may wish to use only a particular selection of the tools discussed. In chapter 5 we learn about a management tool that enables a company to monitor its progress in establishing alignment of strategies. But first, in the next chapter a tool is discussed that will enable a company to evaluate its inventions properly at the various decision stages. As said earlier, having a proper invention evaluation system in place is a first requirement for establishing alignment of strategies.

4
Evaluating Inventions

The future success of technology-based companies relies on their ability to develop new products and services, and inventions are therefore essential to these companies. For that reason, many of these companies are directing large R&D efforts into the development of new inventions, and for many of these inventions patent protection is being sought. However, seeking patent protection for an invention is relatively expensive and should therefore be done only in respect of inventions that are of sufficient importance to the company. Hence, it is very important for a company to develop criteria that would enable the company to distinguish the strategically important inventions and inventions that are potentially of strategic importance from the relatively unimportant inventions.

Strategic Inventions

It is well appreciated that inventions are an important part of a company's intangible assets, and it would therefore make sense to assume that inventions of strategic importance are part of the strategic intangible assets. In this context, the strategic intangible assets, and thus the strategic inventions, are found at the intersection of the three circles in figure 4.1, which model is based on Hubert Saint-Onges' intellectual capital model,[1] using Karl-Erik Sveiby's terminology.[2] The inventions of strategic importance are those inventions that matter most to the company. They are of (potential) commercial relevance, are owned by the company and can ideally be developed in-house, and are supported by the company's infrastructure.

In figure 4.1, employee competence is the sum of the competence, know-how, and skills of the company's employees; it is that which leaves the office at five o'clock in the afternoon and is not owned by the company. In terms of invention evaluation, it reflects a company's understanding of the technical scope of the invention, the company's progress toward commercialization, and the company's ability to develop the technology commercially in-house. Internal structure includes all the company's databases, written procedures, intellectual

Employee Competence   External Structure

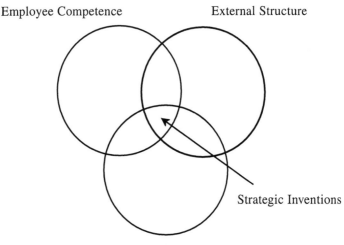

Strategic Inventions

Internal Structure

Figure 4.1
Intangible Assets

assets such as technologies that have been codified and intellectual
property rights, and its infrastructure. In terms of invention evaluation,
it is the scope of protection provided, the patentability of the
invention, and the size of the related existing patent portfolio. External
structure includes a company's relationships with suppliers and
customers, its reputation, the company's understanding of the needs
and wishes of its customers, and the company's position vis-à-vis
competitors. In terms of invention evaluation, it includes the potential
use and impact of an invention in the marketplace, the competitors'
interest, and the possible enforceability of the related patent rights,
once these have been granted.

For efficiency reasons, a company should concentrate only on
those inventions that are of strategic importance and those that are of
potential interest to the company. Inventions of insufficient business
interest should quickly be identified, and at least for the time being, no
further patent action should be taken in respect of these inventions.
Unnecessary costs and time expenditures could thus be avoided, and
it would allow a patent department to focus on the most important
matters.

It should be noted, however, that the evaluation of an invention is always done at a particular moment in time, and what is considered important today could be of less interest at some stage in the future, and of course the other way around. Hence, one can determine the potential value of an invention only at a particular moment in time.

Alignment of Strategies

Obviously, a company's R&D effort should support the company's business objectives and strategy, or put in strategic terms, a company's R&D objectives and strategy should be aligned with the business strategy and objectives. In the ideal world, all the company's inventions, products of its R&D efforts, would be of strategic importance. However, in reality this will not always be the case, and it is therefore necessary to evaluate all the inventions of the company.

In turn, a company's patent activities should support both the business and R&D objectives and strategies, and therefore these activities, as far as inventions are concerned, should focus on inventions of potential importance and those of strategic importance only.

Some Prerequisites

The evaluation of inventions is usually a difficult task to carry out. It is often not as "black and white" as one would wish, and as said earlier, the (potential) importance of an invention may well change in the course of time.

The development of a set of criteria that would enable a company to distinguish potentially important inventions and strategically important inventions from relatively unimportant inventions would therefore be most useful. When one wishes to develop a practical set of evaluation criteria, it appears that the following basic requirements need to be met:

- The criteria should be as simple as possible.
- The set of criteria needs to be endorsed by the business.
- All inventions need to be evaluated by a panel of representatives of the business, R&D, and IP functions.
- The usefulness of the evaluation criteria should be periodically reviewed.

Proposed Set of Evaluation Criteria

On the basis of figure 4.1 and the requirement to have alignment of strategies, the following set of evaluation criteria for determining the potential relevance of an invention is proposed:

Employee Competence

Understanding of the Technical Scope of the Invention

- Complete understanding of the technical scope ☐ (5)
- The boundaries of the technical concept are recognized ☐ (4)
- General idea of the technical concept ☐ (3)
- Some experimental data show an interesting technical effect ☐ (2)
- No technical data are yet available ☐ (1)

Amount of Work Still to be Done before Commercial Implementation

- Invention is commercially used/can be commercialized shortly ☐ (5)
- Prototype has been successful ☐ (4)
- Prototype has been developed ☐ (3)
- Further R&D is encouraged ☐ (2)
- No R&D budget has been made available ☐ (1)

Ability to Develop and Implement the Technology

- Extension of existing product line ☐ (5)
- Related products have been developed ☐ (4)
- Familiar technology ☐ (3)
- Investment needed to acquire development skills ☐ (2)
- Unfamiliar and complex technology ☐ (1)

Internal Structure

Patentability

- Both clearly novel and inventive ☐ (5)

- Clearly novel, and inventive step can be well argued   ☐ (4)
- Novel, and inventive step is arguable   ☐ (3)
- Novel, evidence for inventive step may yet become available   ☐ (2)
- Novel, but evidence for inventive step is not and will not become available   ☐ (1)

Scope of Protection

- Competition cannot circumvent the claims when using same/similar technology   ☐ (5)
- Claims cover all the embodiments of the invention currently known   ☐ (4)
- Competition needs to engineer around the claims   ☐ (3)
- Some protection, but no real blocking power   ☐ (2)
- No useful protection; competition can easily circumvent the claims   ☐ (1)

Related Patent Position

- No protection for related technology   ☐ (5)
- Protection only for commercially used technologies   ☐ (4)
- Moderate portfolio for both defensive and offensive purposes   ☐ (3)
- Extensive patent portfolio that is comparable with major competitors   ☐ (2)
- Leading position in the marketplace   ☐ (1)

External Structure

Proof of Infringement

- Without any problem   ☐ (5)
- Relatively easy without major efforts   ☐ (4)
- Possible but requires a clear effort   ☐ (3)
- Difficult and requiring major efforts   ☐ (2)
- Impossible to prove   ☐ (1)

Attractiveness for Competitors

- It is essential for their businesses to have access to
  this technology   ☐ (5)
- Of high interest since it will affect their competitive
  position   ☐ (4)
- Of interest but they are exploring other directions   ☐ (3)
- Of little interest because of low financial impact   ☐ (2)
- Of no interest   ☐ (1)

Alternative Technology

- **This technology will set a new standard**   ☐ **(5)**
- The technology has major advantages over existing
  alternatives   ☐ (4)
- Various compatible technologies are available   ☐ (3)
- No alternative is available yet, but is likely to be
  developed shortly   ☐ (2)
- A superior alternative is available   ☐ (1)

Alignment of Strategies

**In-House Business Interest and Support to
Commercialize the Invention**

- Technology is a top priority within the company   ☐ (5)
- Strong commitment/support to develop the technology
  further   ☐ (4)
- Competitive advantage expected   ☐ (3)
- Further R&D expenditure allowed   ☐ (2)
- In conflict with the company's business objectives   ☐ (1)

Cost Savings

- **Provides the company a substantial competitive**
  advantage   ☐ (5)
- Improves the competitive position of the company   ☐ (4)
- Cost savings are questionable   ☐ (3)
- Consolidates the company's position   ☐ (2)
- More expensive than existing products   ☐ (1)

Revenue Impact (For example by Product and Service Differentiation)

- Changes the competitive position of the company substantially ☐ (5)
- Clearly improves the company's competitive position ☐ (4)
- Revenue increase is questionable ☐ (3)
- Will not have an impact on current revenues ☐ (2)
- Deteriorating effect on current revenues ☐ (1)

In respect of each of these four areas of business interest, that is, employee competence, internal structure, external structure, and alignment of strategies, an "average" potential value (score) can be determined from the respective criteria, ranging from 1 to 5. Depending on the technology concerned, the strategic objectives of the business, and the nature of the company in question, some evaluation criteria may be considered of strategically higher importance than others. Hence, in determining the average values, the strategic relevance of each criterion in a particular area of business interest needs to be assessed and to be taken into account. For instance, in respect of the area of external structure, a company making a great out-licensing effort may wish to put greater weight on "attractiveness for competitors" than on the other related criteria. Thus, the criterion of "attractiveness for competitors" could, for instance, have a strategic weight of 2, whereas the other criteria of "alternative technology" and "proof of infringement" may both have a strategic weight of 1. It will be clear that such strategic weights should be allocated in close consultation with the business and R&D functions.

In addition, the impact of negative scores should be considered carefully to determine whether they would outdo or offset positive scores of other criteria. It is further recognized that some companies may wish to use alternative criteria for the four areas of business interest, reflecting their particular circumstances and strategic objectives more adequately. From the average potential values of the four areas of business interest, the final potential value of the invention can be determined, ranging from 1 to 5. In determining the final potential value of the invention, the strategic relevance of each of the four areas of business interest also needs to be considered and taken into account, because for some companies they may differ from one to another.

Further, some companies may consider the set of fixed descriptions for each score to be too rigid, not sufficiently taking into account the uncertainties involved in evaluating inventions. These companies could use the same scoring ranges for the criteria (1 to 5), without considering the fixed set of descriptions. From experience, it would appear, however, that often representatives of the various functions prefer to have (at least some) guidance on how to allocate scores, so as to understand what a particular score would mean in practice. This is especially the case when many evaluation decisions need to be taken by a variety of persons, and one wishes to ensure a consistent evaluation throughout the patent portfolio.

Within this range the following categories of potential value (pv) are identified:

- pv = 5; these inventions are considered of high strategic importance.
- pv = 4; these inventions are considered of strategic importance.
- pv = 3; these inventions are considered of potential importance.
- pv = 2; these inventions are considered of limited potential importance.
- pv = 1; these inventions are considered of no importance.

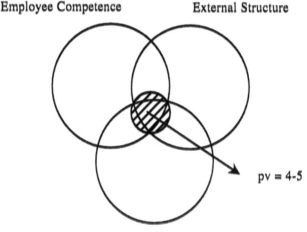

Figure 4.2
Inventions of Strategic Importance

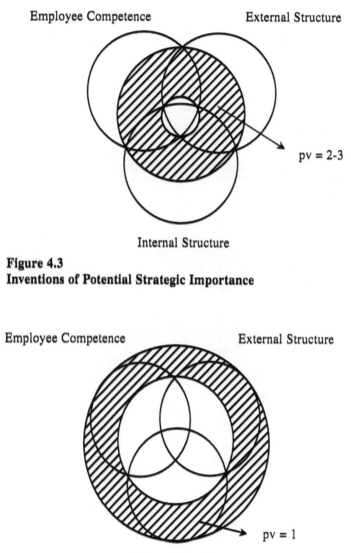

Employee Competence

External Structure

pv = 2-3

Internal Structure

Figure 4.3
Inventions of Potential Strategic Importance

Employee Competence

External Structure

pv = 1

Internal Structure

Figure 4.4
Inventions of Insufficient (Nonstrategic) Importance

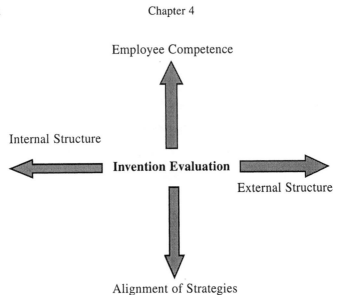

Figure 4.5
Effective Invention Evaluation

These five categories can subsequently be separated into three main categories of inventions:

- Those of strategic importance, pv = 4-5 (see figure 4.2)
- Those of potential strategic importance, pv = 2-3 (see figure 4.3)
- Those of insufficient (nonstrategic) importance, pv = 1 (see figure 4.4)

Such a distinction would make sense from a business perspective, since the invention evaluation is based on the three essential areas of business interest, namely, employee competence, internal structure, and external structure and on the requirement that there should exist alignment of strategies (see figure 4.5).

The potential value reflects the strategic relevance or relative irrelevance of the invention concerned. The higher the value, the more important the invention will be for the company. In addition, it reflects the need for a proper balance between the three areas of business interest. A high score in only one area or moderate scores in some areas will normally not be enough. An invention of (potential) strategic importance needs to score relatively high in various areas, thus reflecting that the invention has commercial relevance, is owned by the company, and is supported by the company's infrastructure, and that a patent right covering the invention would have sufficient blocking power.

For instance, an invention may be very successful from a scientific point of view. Its patentability and scope of protection may be high, and the technical scope may be fully understood. However, if there would be no business support to develop the invention into a commercial product, because of lack of interest in the marketplace or the availability of commercially more attractive technology, the invention is only of very limited interest to the company.

Equally, a company can be highly committed to support inventions and to develop them into commercial products, and may have the infrastructure and the financial strength to do so. However, the company also needs to have a proper understanding of the technical scope of the invention, if it wishes to obtain useful patent protection that could provide a competitive edge. In addition, the patent rights covering the invention should have enough blocking power, and the invention needs, of course, to be of (potential) commercial relevance.

Further, there might potentially be a high demand for a particular product in the marketplace. However, to be of value to the company, a related invention needs to be owned (at least partly) by the company, related patent rights should have enough blocking power, the company should understand the technical scope of the invention, and ideally it should be in the position to develop the invention into a commercial product in-house.

Moreover, inventions that do not support the company's business objectives and strategy are likely to receive no support within the company, as no commercial business relevance will be perceived.

Various Evaluation Stages

From a patent perspective, there are three stages when the potential value of an invention needs to be determined:

- The review and first filing stage
- The foreign filing stage
- The maintenance decision stage

Often, the real potential of an invention may become clear only after a while. Further R&D work and marketing surveys may, for example, be required to reinforce the significance of the invention, or disappointing data from further experimental work or marketing surveys may bring about a loss of interest in the possible commercialization of the invention. Regular evaluation is therefore essential, if one wishes to manage a patent portfolio cost-effectively and efficiently.

The above set of evaluation criteria can be used at each of these three stages. The respective final values obtained could, for instance, show a decrease or increase in the potential value of a particular invention. On the basis of the final value in each stage, a relatively simple decision-making process is proposed for each of these stages.

Review and First Filing Stage

- pv = 4-5: filing clearly justified
- pv = 2-3: filing is justified
- pv = 1: no filing (yet)

In case of pv = 1, it could be concluded that no drafting and filing need to take place yet. It may, for instance, be the case that further experimental data are required, or that internal business support has yet to emerge, or that (potential) interest in the marketplace is not yet clear. However, it may well be that further information could become available in due course that would justify a reconsideration of the earlier decision not to file. Alternatively, one could decide to just publish the invention for defensive purposes.

Foreign Filing Stage

- pv = 4-5: extensive foreign filing
- pv = 2-3: limited foreign filing
- pv = 1: no foreign filing

In principle, this means that there could exist two standard foreign filing programs, a limited program and a more extensive program. However, it could be decided to establish separate foreign filing programs for each of the categories 2-5, allowing a greater variety in foreign filing programs.

Alternatively, a company could take a more robust approach toward its cases of limited potential interest and decide that such cases should not be first filed or foreign filed.

Maintenance Decision Stage

As said earlier, the true potential of an invention is often not known from the outset, however, this changes in the course of time. It makes sense therefore, at the review and first filing stage as well as the foreign filing stage, to continue also with the cases of potential importance. The simple reason being that such an invention of potential importance may well turn into a strategically important invention, and one can simply not run the risk of having no protection for a new business opportunity.

Maintenance decisions, on the other hand, are usually made in respect of cases that are a particular number of years old. For instance, maintenance exercises can be organized annually in respect of cases that are older than three years. As one can expect, in the course of time much more will be known about the true potential of a particular invention. In times of relatively short product life cycles and a rapidly changing business environment, the true potential of an invention should be more clear at the maintenance stage than at the review and first filing stage or foreign filing stage. One must at the maintenance stage be in a better position to distinguish the cases that will support the interim and long-term business objectives and strategy from those that will not.

In addition, maintenance decisions have generally a greater financial impact than first filing and foreign filing decisions. Hence, one should take a firmer stance regarding the potential value of an invention at the maintenance stage than at the previous two decision stages.

Because nonstrategic inventions do not support the interim and long-term business objectives and strategy, incurring costs instead of adding value to the company, they should be abandoned at an early stage.

A prerequisite is, of course, that the maintenance decision makers —the panel of business, R&D, and IP representatives—should be well aware of the strategic objectives of the company. Their decisions need to reflect the business objectives in a consistent manner.

Further, to facilitate a useful maintenance decision process (the same applies to the two earlier decision stages), one also needs to have a proper understanding of the marketplace, not only in respect of one's own activities, but especially in respect of competitors' activities and intentions.

In view of the above, the following maintenance decision process could be proposed:

- pv = 4-5: to be maintained
- pv = 3: to be maintained, at least for the time being
- pv = 1-2: to be abandoned

It is advisable to indicate in respect of each decision the objective of filing or maintaining the case (e.g., exclusivity, licensing, or freedom of action).

Licensing

From a licensing perspective, there are two important reasons for a company to have patent rights:

- Generation of licensing income
- Avoidance of licensing fees by way of cross-license agreements

Many companies put much effort into what is called the "mining" of patent portfolios with the aim of finding "golden nuggets" that can be leveraged by licensing activities. It will be clear that those golden nuggets or key patents can be identified by means of the above described set of invention evaluation criteria.

It will be clear that category pv = 5 represents the company's key patents. Such identification could be very useful for enforcement and stick licensing purposes, or carrot licensing if the company would be prepared to license strategically important (core) technology to others. Clearly, the company's licensing activities need to support the business objectives, and it is therefore important to develop a licensing strategy that indicates the categories of patent assets that can be licensed to others and the particular objectives involved. In addition, it could identify the technology that the company needs to license from others.

Obviously, before abandoning a nonstrategic invention, possible rights of third parties should be identified and addressed, and the carrot licensing potential of the invention should be determined.

Conclusion

In this chapter, a set of evaluation criteria has been discussed that enables a company to distinguish the more important inventions from the less important inventions. The set of criteria facilitates alignment of strategies and allows a company to reach informed business decisions at the various decision stages. In addition, the evaluation criteria enable a company to mine the patent portfolio for licensing purposes. In the next chapter, the management of a patent portfolio will be brought to a higher level. There, we will see how the performance of a company's patent assets can be measured and the alignment of strategies can be monitored.

Notes

1. In Saint-Onges' model, intellectual capital is defined as the sum of human capital (the capabilities of the individuals required to provide solutions to customers), structural capital (the organizational capabilities of the organization to meet market requirements), and customer capital (the depth, width, attachment, and profitability of the franchise). The interdependence of these three components is usually shown in a diagram that resembles figure 4.1. See Patrick H. Sullivan, *Profiting from Intellectual Capital, Extracting Value from Innovation* (New York: John Wiley & Sons, Inc., 1998), 5 and 207.
2. Sveiby defines intangible assets to consist of three components, namely, employee competence (education, experience), internal structure (the organization: management, legal structure, manual systems, attitudes, R&D, software), and external structure (brands, customer and supplier relations). See Karl Erik Sveiby, *The New Organizational Wealth, Managing and Measuring Knowledge-based Assets* (San Francisco: Berrett-Koehler Publishers, Inc., 1997), 2 and 12. In this book also the terms employee competence, internal structure, and external structure are used (although they cover slightly different things), because it is felt that these terms effectively reflect the three areas of intangible assets that are relevant for inventions and patents.

5

Measuring the Performance of a Company's Patent Assets

Since patent assets are becoming increasingly important strategic business tools, making or breaking technology-based companies, effective patent asset management is becoming key to the future success of these companies. A frequently observed problem within patent departments, however, is that because of the already heavy, let alone increasing, workload, there is often insufficient time to adequately manage patent portfolios. Indeed, many patent departments are too busy with the day-to-day professional activities such as drafting, filing, prosecution, counseling activities, and so forth, and they do not have the time to take a step back to review and measure the performance of their patent portfolios.

For various reasons this is an undesirable situation.

First, patent rights are expensive to obtain and maintain, and thus there is every reason to measure the performance of these assets. Questions every company should address include: Is the investment in these assets justified? What do they add to the company's bottom line? What is their return on investment? These questions are easily asked but quite difficult to answer. Nonetheless, in times when profit margins are increasingly under pressure as a result of a more aggressive and truly global competition, these matters need to be addressed. The fact that patent assets are generally becoming more important should not give a patent department a free hand to file as many patent applications as possible. Companies can easily be trapped in a rat race of filing more patent applications than competitors.

Second, in addition to the immediate costs of obtaining and maintaining patent rights, such a filing policy could potentially cost a company unjustifiable amounts of money in the long term, since a situation could arise wherein the company no longer knows which patent assets it actually owns and for what particular purpose.

Strategic Patent Assets

Patent assets are an important component of a company's intellectual assets, and it therefore makes sense to consider the strategic patent assets to be part of the strategic intellectual assets, those intellectual assets that matter commercially most to the company. As we have seen in the previous chapter, the strategic intellectual assets are found at the intersection of the three circles in figure 5.1. In the context of patent assets, employee competence is a company's capability to develop new technology that can be protected by patent rights; internal structure is a company's complete patent portfolio and related administration; and external structure includes the use and impact of a company's patent portfolio in the marketplace.

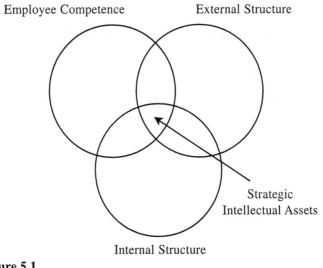

Figure 5.1
Intangible Assets

To be efficient and effective, a company should in its day-to-day operations concentrate only on the patent assets that really matter, that is, the strategic patent assets, those patent assets that support both the business and R&D strategies and objectives. Nonstrategic patent assets do not support a company's business objectives; they incur costs and do not add to the bottom line of a company. Therefore, a company's aim should be to focus its patent activities on strategic patent assets only. In this context, patent assets covering noncore technology that are licensed to others are also considered strategic patent assets. This means that ideally a company's patent portfolio should consist of strategic patent assets only.

Unfortunately, however, this is usually not the case, hence, the need to evaluate a company's complete patent portfolio, including possibly nonstrategic patent assets, and related activities. Only then can a proper picture be obtained of the performance of a company's patent assets and their management. As we have seen before, such evaluation can be carried out by way of a patent assets audit during which, and in consultation with business and R&D personnel, the business relevance of each of the patent assets is considered, thus ensuring that an informed business decision can be made in respect of each individual patent asset. In this way, one obtains a proper understanding of what the patent portfolio is all about, and the performance of the company's patent assets can be measured. However, before a patent portfolio can properly be evaluated and the performance of the patent assets can be assessed, the business, R&D, and patent strategies should be known, and, of course, these strategies need to be aligned.

Alignment of Strategies

As we have seen earlier, a company's patent strategy should be aligned with both a company's R&D and business objectives and strategies, whereas the R&D strategy needs to be aligned with the business strategy. A company's patent strategy consists of the company's efforts to make sure that its patent activities support the business, that is, to ensure that the patent activities are focused on newly developed and strategic technology originating from a company's R&D efforts and strategic technology already owned by the company.

Alignment of these strategies may sound obvious, but it needs careful consideration if one for instance wants to avoid developing commercially useless products, creating nonstrategic patent assets covering the wrong technology, or commercializing new technology without proper patent protection. The alignment of these strategies and their interdependence is shown in figure 5.2. Obviously, these strategies need to be reviewed periodically, so as to keep them up to date.

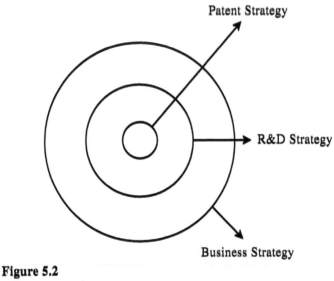

Patent Strategy

R&D Strategy

Business Strategy

Figure 5.2
Alignment of Strategies

Using the model in figure 5.1, it can be said that a business strategy focuses on society, business environment, its customers, the company itself, and the way it works to realize its objectives and vision. In other words, it embraces all of a company's intangible assets (see figure 5.3). A company's R&D strategy is that part of a company's business strategy that focuses on the development of technology required to achieve the business objectives and embraces the intangible assets only as far as they are linked into R&D efforts (see figure 5.4). A company's patent strategy focuses on the strategic technology either newly developed or already owned by the company and embraces the strategic intellectual assets (see figure 5.5).

Evaluation Indices and Measurement Indicators

The valuation of a company's patent assets is a tricky business, as everyone will agree who has given it some thought and spent time on such an effort. One of the reasons is that the accounting methods do not exist to enable people to come up with an accurate estimate of the economic value of a company's patent assets, as for instance is the

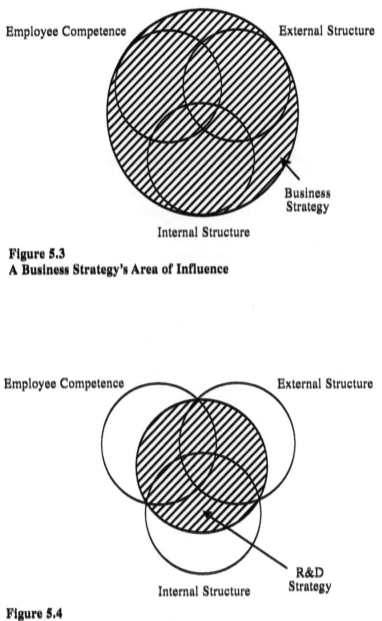

Employee Competence

External Structure

Business
Strategy

Internal Structure

Figure 5.3
A Business Strategy's Area of Influence

Employee Competence

External Structure

Internal Structure

R&D
Strategy

Figure 5.4
A R&D Strategy's Area of Influence

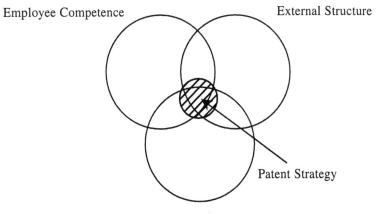

Employee Competence   External Structure

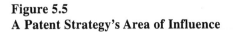

Patent Strategy

Internal Structure

Figure 5.5
A Patent Strategy's Area of Influence

case for tangible assets. In addition, a company can file patent applications for different strategic reasons that may require different
methods to valuate the patent assets in question.

It is therefore not without reason that much focus is on the evaluation of the relative performance of patent assets rather than on the
assessment of the economic value of patent assets in absolute terms.
In practice, this means that evaluation indices and measurement indicators are being developed with the aim of monitoring the performance of a company's patent assets and their management. Although
evaluation indices or measurement indicators do not provide an
adequate assessment of the economic value of patent assets, they
nonetheless can be most useful instruments to identify over time the
areas of potential risk, particular trends, and areas of necessary
change. In addition, goals or targets and permitted deviation ranges
could be attached to indices and indicators, ensuring that the
company's patent activities will be aligned with the business goals of
the company.

Some Prerequisites

When one wishes to develop a set of evaluation indices and measurement indicators for a company's patent assets and their management, there appear to be some basic requirements one needs to meet to come up with a practical set of indices and indicators.

First, it needs to be clear what the precise aim is of having such a set of evaluation indices and measurement indicators. Usually, the aim is to provide top management of a company with knowledge regarding the state of affairs of the company's patent assets, for example, the extent to which these assets are aligned with corporate goals, thus enabling management decisions to be made at the highest level in the company and ensuring that patent assets are indeed used as strategic business tools. In addition, appropriately edited information might usefully be made available to shareholders.

For that reason, a set of evaluation indices and measurement indicators should be kept as simple as possible. In practice, that will not always be easy, but simplicity is what needs to be aimed at, especially since top managers are not likely to be experts in patents. Periodic reports should be concise, easy to understand, and should reflect ideally in a nutshell the performance of a company's patent assets and their management.

Second, the whole exercise of developing a set of evaluation indices and measurement indicators needs to be done in close consultation with top management and business personnel. The reasons are that the exercise needs support from top management since it may cost considerable management time and that quite a lot of commercial information will be needed from business personnel. Not only that, but top management also needs to be committed at the outset of the exercise and be prepared to act on the information obtained from the evaluation indices and measurement indicators, whereas business personnel need to understand the process involved, its objectives, and what it means to their business.

Third, and as said earlier, for a proper evaluation, a company's complete patent portfolio and related activities need to be reviewed. Only then can the company determine whether there exists alignment between the business, R&D, and patent strategies.

Proposed Set of Evaluation Indices
And Measurement Indicators

On the basis of figures 5.1-5.5, a model of evaluation indices and
measurement indicators for a company's patent assets and their
management is proposed, for a particular period of time (most likely
once every year), broken down in the following areas:

Employee Competence

*   Number of reported inventions (of substance)/R&D employee
*   Number of first filings/R&D employee
*   Number of inventions foreign filed/R&D employee
*   Number of inventors/number of reported inventions (of
    substance)

These indices reflect the innovativeness of R&D staff, the extent
to which a company may be dependent on key individuals for developing new technology, and the potential relevance of new inventions.

Internal Structure

*   Average age per patent right (years)
*   Percentage of patented inventions not yet published
*   Total number of patent rights
*   Total number of patented inventions
*   Number of first filings
*   Number of inventions foreign filed

These indices and indicators indicate the size of the patent
portfolio, its maturity, its growth and renewal, and the extent to which
global protection is sought.

External Structure

*   Percentage of patented inventions commercially used by the
    company
*   Percentage of patented inventions licensed to others
*   Percentage of patented inventions involved in disputes

- Percentage of total patent department time spent on patent rights owned by others

These indices visualize the extent to which the patent portfolio is used in the marketplace. They further reveal the need to look at other companies, including immediate competitors, as potential customers. In addition, they visualize the potential business relevance of a company's patent assets in the marketplace. Further, they may show the possible imbalance between a company's patent activities and those of others.

Alignment of Strategies

- Percentage of total sales protected by patent rights
- Percentage of total income from licensing patent rights
- Percentage of new-to-market products/services protected by patent rights
- Sales protected by patent rights/R&D expenditure
- Licensing income from patent rights/R&D expenditure
- Total patent costs/R&D expenditure

These indices visualize the effectiveness of patent assets as strategic business tools, the extent to which a company's patent strategy is aligned with its business and R&D strategies. They further indicate the effectiveness of a company's R&D effort to create strategic patent assets. In addition, these indices visualize the effectiveness of a company's patent assets management.

The company's patent strategy is central to the model (see figure 5.6). The evaluation indices and measurement indicators should directly link into the company's patent strategy, or put differently, the activities represented by the indices and indicators should be emphasized in the patent strategy. The values of these indices and indicators reflect the company's performance in respect of the various patent activities. Goals, targets, and permitted deviation ranges can be attached to the indices and indicators, showing in a nutshell what the patent strategy is all about and how alignment of strategies is to be realized. Actions may need to be taken and initiatives may need to be developed by the patent department and other parts of the business to ensure that goals and targets are met or that

Employee Competence

Internal Structure

 **Patent Strategy**

External Structure

Alignment of Strategies

Figure 5.6
Effective Measurement of the Performance of Patent Assets

the values fall within the permitted deviation ranges.

The values of the indices and indicators need to be determined and considered periodically, at least once a year. In respect of each of these indices and indicators an age curve can be drawn, showing any development/change in the value of the index or indicator in question over a period of time. Such age curves will enable a company to identify particular trends, potential areas of risk, and possible inconsistencies between the patent strategy and the business and R&D strategies in a timely manner, allowing the company to act swiftly on the information obtained from the model.

Create Your Own Model

The above model will enable a company to manage its patent assets in an effective manner. It is recognized, however, that some companies may have difficulty with the relatively high number of indices and indicators (twenty in total). Those companies could select from the above model the key indices and indicators of their choice. The following set of key indices and indicators could for instance be useful for a company not having a strong out-licensing strategy:

Employee Competence

* Number of reported inventions (of substance)/R&D employee
* Number of inventors/number of reported inventions (of substance)

Internal Structure

* Average age per patent right (years)
* Total number of patent rights
* Total number of patented inventions

External Structure

* Percentage of patented inventions commercially used by the company
* Percentage of patented inventions involved in disputes

Alignment of Strategies

* Percentage of total sales protected by patent rights
* Percentage of new-to-market products/services protected by patent rights
* Sales protected by patent rights/R&D expenditure

Although a more concise set of key indices and indicators could possibly be more "user-friendly" and still provide sufficient information to manage patent assets effectively, it is clear that the twenty indices/indicators will give a more complete picture of the performance of a company's patent assets and their management.

Other companies may wish to use different indices and indicators that could reflect their particular circumstances and patent strategies more adequately. The following alternative indices and indicators could, for instance, be considered:

Employee Competence

- Number of reported inventions
- Number of reported inventions/employee
- Number of first filings/employee
- Number of inventions foreign filed/employee
- Number of new filings (published)/employee
- Number of new filings (published)/R&D employee
- Number of inventors/number of reported inventions
- Percentage of total patent department time spent on educating and training business and R&D staff on intellectual property
- Growth in number of reported inventions (percentage)
- Patent citation index
- Number of key inventors

Internal Structure

- Number of key inventions
- Number of filings of strategic patent assets
- Number of nonstrategic patent assets abandoned
- Percentage of patented inventions that are key inventions
- Percentage of patent assets abandoned
- Percentage of patent assets first filed
- Percentage of new patent assets drafted by outside counsel
- Total outside counsel costs/total patent costs
- Number of patent assets acquired
- Number of patent assets sold
- Patent staff retention rate
- Average time between report of invention and filing of patent application
- Average cost of patent application

External Structure

- Number of patented inventions licensed to others
- Number of patented inventions licensed from others
- Percentage of total patent expenditure spent on patent rights owned by others
- Success rate in enforcement actions
- Success rate in attacking patent rights owned by others

- Percentage of total patent department time spent on defending patent rights

Alignment of Strategies

- Total sales/R&D expenditure
- Licensing income from patent rights/licensing center costs
- Licensing balance (out-licensing/in-licensing)
- Percentage of total patent department time spent on multifunctional intellectual asset management (IAM) team activities
- Percentage of total patent department time spent on reviewing/filing procedures
- Total patent fees/total patent costs
- Percentage of patented inventions of strategic importance
- Percentage of patented inventions of potential strategic importance
- Total sales/patented invention
- Total sales/patent asset
- R&D expenditure/patented invention
- R&D expenditure/patent asset

The Model in Practice

To provide a feel for how one can work with the model in practice, we will consider two companies, A and B, long-standing competitors in the same area of business. Their respective evaluation indices and measurement indicators for 2003 are shown in table 4.1, and these are discussed for each area herein below.

Employee Competence

Although the patentability of company A's new inventions may be higher than that of company B (company A foreign files more reported inventions), company B seems to be more innovative. Not only does company B generate more potential inventions (more reported inventions of substance per R&D employee), but it also involves more staff in the process of developing new inventions (more inventors among R&D staff). On the other hand, company A seems to rely much more on a limited number of staff, which could prove risky in case the regular inventor(s) retires or changes job.

Internal Structure

Company A clearly has a problem. When compared with company B, its source for new inventions is running dry, whereas at the same time its patent portfolio seems to age quickly (small number of first filings for company A, small number of not yet published patent rights, and a high average age per patent right). Further, company B is filing its patented inventions more broadly, which could make sense in view of today's business globalization (for company B the average size per patent family is much larger).

External Structure

It may well be a deliberate strategy of company A not to license to others; the limited business relevance of its patent assets in the marketplace, however, suggests that its technology is much more mature than that of company B, thus confirming our earlier finding that company A may indeed have a problem (company A's patent portfolio is commercially used to greater extent, but there seems to be little patent activity in this field by others).

Alignment of Strategies

Company A has more than one problem when compared with company B. Relying on mature technology is one thing; doing nothing about such a situation is a different matter (maturity of technology is suggested by the high sales protected by patents rights). As indicated earlier, company A seems not very successful in developing new technology that is of commercial relevance (very few new-to-market products/services protected by patent rights). Its limited R&D expenditure—when compared with company B—could well explain this. Further, the relatively high patent costs for company A seem to confirm the view that its patent portfolio would cover mature, and more likely superseded, technology. It seems good timing for company A to carry out a patent assets audit and to bring its R&D and patent strategies in line with its business strategy and objectives, if it has any.

In view of the above, it is likely that company A will be a loser in the not too distant future, whereas company B may well be a winner. One thing is clear, however; if company A wants to be successful or survive in the future, it needs to address the problems identified with the model. Indeed, if company A would realize its actual condition, it would need to implement drastic changes shortly. A possible option could well be to acquire the required new technology elsewhere, by way of strategic alliance, merger, or acquisition. The good news for company A is that a proper patent mapping exercise could identify company B as a possible candidate to acquire or merge with, since most of the internal structure patent information is publicly available today.

Conclusion

In this chapter, a model of evaluation indices and measurement indicators has been discussed that enables a company to measure the performance of its patent assets. Although some of the conclusions drawn from the information provided by the individual indices and indicators may be subject to debate, overall the model enables the appropriate identification of particular trends and potential areas of risk. It further enables a company to determine the extent to which a company's patent strategy is aligned with its business and R&D strategies and objectives and allows a company to consider possible actions that may need to be taken to accomplish alignment of the strategies in a timely manner. Moreover, consideration of the indices and indicators will trigger the sort of questions that need to be addressed if a company wishes to manage its patent assets effectively.

The development and implementation of this tool—but this applies equally to all the tools that have been discussed in the previous chapters—requires an active attitude of a patent department, a new IP culture with greater emphasis on value creation and extraction. In the next chapter, we learn how such a new IP culture can be created.

Table 4.1. Year 2003

Indices / Indicators	Company A	Company B
Employee Competence		
• Number of reported inventions (of substance)/ R&D employee	0.1	0.3
• Number of first filings/R&D employee	0.075	0.15
• Number of inventions foreign filed/R&D employee	0.075	0.10
• Number of inventors/number of reported inventions (of substance)	0.02	0.15
Internal Structure		
• Average age per patent right (years)	16	9
• Percentage of patented inventions not yet published	4%	20%
• Total number of patent rights	10,000	15,000
• Total number of patented inventions	1,000	1,000
• Number of first filings	15	100
• Number of inventions foreign filed	15	67
External Structure		
• Percentage of patented inventions commercially used by the company	7%	14%
• Percentage of patented inventions licensed to others	-	15%
• Percentage of patented inventions involved in disputes	0.5%	5%
• Percentage of total patent department time spent on patent rights owned by others	5%	25%
Alignment of strategies		
• Percentage of total sales protected by patent rights	50%	30%
• Percentage of total income from licensing patent rights	-	0.8%
• Percentage of new-to-market products/services protected by patent rights	10%	95%
• Sales protected by patent rights/R&D expenditure	10.0	6.0
• Licensing income from patent rights/R&D expenditure	-	0.2
• Total patent costs/R&D expenditure (%)	4%	2%

6
Creating a New IP Culture

Intellectual capital is likely to dominate the IP world in the near future because it is the new wave of interest in the business world to put intellectual property rights, and especially patents, high up on corporate agendas. It is therefore prudent for patent professionals to be aware of this development, especially since they will be affected by it. To prepare patent professionals for the intellectual capital era in which patents will become increasingly important business tools, a new IP culture is called for, one with greater emphasis on value creation and extraction. However, before we show how such a new IP culture can be created, the intellectual capital concept will be briefly discussed to enable patent professionals to understand the need for this new culture.

The Intellectual Capital Concept

What is intellectual capital? In financial terms, it is the difference between the market value and the book value of a company, or as some put it, it is the value of a company's intangible assets, that value of the company that is not found in balance sheets of a company, in the past often referred to as "goodwill." If, however, intellectual capital is thought of as being the value of a company's intangible assets, it is important to note that this value is not just the sum of all the intangibles; it also includes the ability to transform the intangibles into financial gain. It is not without reason that intellectual capital is often referred to as "knowledge that can be converted into profits."[1]

Today, the intangible assets of a company often outdo its tangible assets, something that is reflected in the significant, and sometimes staggering, difference between the market and book values of a company. However, since conventional accounting methods take only tangible assets into consideration, one can no longer rely on those methods only for an accurate assessment of a company's total value. Therefore, new methods need to be developed to assess a company's intellectual capital in an useful, reliable, and therefore acceptable manner. Reasons for the need of such methods have been well argued.[2]

Methods that are widely accepted by all parties involved, that is, investors, stock market governing bodies, and the businesses themselves, are however not yet available, let alone standardized methods.

A pioneer in this field is Skandia, the Scandinavian insurance and finance company. In 1995, it was the first company to present a supplement on intellectual capital to its annual report.[3] Since then, Skandia's valuation has gone up considerably, one of the reasons being that investors believe in Skandia's ability to prosper from its intellectual capital in the future.

Measuring the value of a company's intangible assets and providing the related information to the financial world is just one way of creating a competitive advantage in the marketplace. Equally, if not more, important, a reliable assessment of the value of the company's intangible assets enables the business to make better decisions in respect of these assets. For a company to be successful in the future, a committed effort will be required to ensure that value will be created for future commercialization and as much value as possible will be extracted from a company's existing intangible assets.

Major Challenges—the Good and the Possible Bad News

The message the intellectual capital concept will have for top management of a company is: there is potentially hidden value in the company, which when discovered and leveraged, will generate more profit. Therefore, CEOs and CFOs will want to look into this new concept, especially when their business margins are already increasingly under pressure due to increased competition on a truly global scale, and rightly so. In the future, there will be only two types of companies: winners and losers. There will be no place for mediocrity. Those companies that will make a committed effort to manage their intellectual capital will be among the winners, but even they should start making such effort sooner rather than later.

Since patent rights are becoming increasingly important to companies, patent professionals will be expected to provide a large contribution to the management of a company's intellectual assets (codified competence, know-how, technology, databases, procedures, and intellectual property rights) to ensure that these patent rights will indeed provide a competitive advantage and add value to the company's bottom line.

There are two major challenges patent professionals may have to face:

- The reliable measurement of the value of the company's patent portfolio
- The management of the patent portfolio with the view to create value that can be leveraged in the future and to extract as much value as possible from the existing portfolio

In the light of this, will the role of patent professionals change in the intellectual capital era? Some patent professionals may think that nothing will change in their work. Various reasonings may apply. In some companies, for instance, intellectual asset management may already have been intrinsically present to some extent. Other patent professionals just may not believe in this new concept of intellectual capital altogether. For the patent professionals belonging to the latter category and those who would not like to be involved in any change, there is bad news. Whether they like it or not, and despite some efforts to ridicule the concept,[4] intellectual capital and thus intellectual asset management have come here to stay, there is no doubt about it.

At present, it seems that the potential impact the intellectual capital concept will have on patent professionals and their work is generally underestimated within the patent profession, although it would appear that U.S. patent professionals are more aware of it than their European colleagues. Obviously, this needs to change. The measurement of the value of patents as such is already a very complicated matter and so is the value extraction from one's patent portfolio. But that is not all; in addition, the relationship of patent professionals with their business colleagues is likely to change considerably.

Dow's Success

Dow Chemical is one of the companies that is making an effort to manage its intellectual assets more effectively. In recent years, it pruned its patent portfolio considerably, thereby saving approximately $40 million in patent maintenance costs over the following ten years, while at the same time it increased its licensing income from $25 million in the mid-1990s to well over \$125 million currently.[5] This is impressive. Cynics will argue that Dow's patent department apparently did not have its act together for many years and that it was about time something was done about it. This is not likely to be the case. These cynics are advised to make an effort and find out what really has been established at Dow,[6] to understand, for instance, what something called the Technology Factor method is all about.[7] It will be an eye-opener to them. Their professional lives will never be the same. Welcome to the club. They will start to realize that intellectual asset management is not just a matter of pruning deadwood from a patent portfolio and making an extra licensing effort. Of course, this helps, but there is much more to it. It involves a paradigm shift, a new way for patent professionals to look at their work, their relationships within the company, and the competition. To be successful, a new culture will need to be established within a patents department, one with more emphasis on value creation and extraction.

Changing Relationships

Once business people realize the increasing value of patent rights, they will have higher expectations of the services provided by patent professionals. In addition, the business is likely to move into the territory conventionally belonging to patent professionals by taking over responsibilities that were previously with the patent professionals only. In this context, it is worth mentioning that traditionally patent professionals consider the patent portfolio to be their "property." It is a matter exclusively dealt with and managed by patent professionals. Some are actually reluctant to share information about patents and related matters with their business colleagues, since they fear that provision of too much information may result in a situation wherein the business people themselves, and without proper consultation of the patents department, will decide on matters such as infringement and validity. Although that concern may be real, it is more likely to say something about a patent department's profile and relationships and communication within a company than anything else.

In the intellectual capital era, patent rights and intellectual property rights in general will become "shared" property within a company. Decisions regarding patent assets will be business decisions or, more accurately, informed business decisions reached in consultation with patent professionals, that is to say, provided that patent professionals have positioned themselves to ensure that they provide the most possible value to the company and that their contribution is recognized by the business. Otherwise, it is likely that the business increasingly will take control of the patent portfolio, and related decisions may be made by the business only, without proper consultation of patent professionals. Consequently, a situation could arise in which patent professionals would mainly be seen as draftsmen for patent applications. In addition, it is likely that business personnel (including finance personnel and strategists) will want to take control of the licensing activities, especially once these activities become increasingly successful and start to create considerable revenues for a company. Without any doubt, such developments could potentially be frustrating for patent professionals, because on the one hand patents will become more important for their company, and consequently their department's profile will rise, whereas at the same time the work of the patent professionals may become less interesting. This may especially apply to U.S. patent attorneys since they are traditionally more involved with licensing activities than for instance their European colleagues. On the other hand, it could be argued that a possible shift of licensing activities from patent professionals to business people would be beneficial for a company. Since licensing work usually involves some urgency, there is the potential risk that a patent professional responsible for both license and patent activities will do the licensing job first, thus possibly delaying the filing of a new and important patent application. Hence, such a shift could possibly have a positive impact on the number of patent filings and the quality of the patent applications, thus contributing to the future success of the company, but is it likely to contribute to the patent professional's job satisfaction? It depends. It may well be that as a result of improved awareness within the business of the value of patent assets, there will be a greater demand from the business for counseling and transactional advice. In addition, patent professionals may receive more feedback from the business, allowing decision-making processes to be more effective and patent professionals to obtain a better understanding of the needs and objectives of the business. If so, a concern for a less interesting job in the future may be unjustified. It is, however, important for patent professionals to be aware of the possibility that a shift may occur in their range of responsibilities.

In view of the changing relationships, a major and immediate challenge for patents departments will be to position themselves in such a way that they add maximum value to the business, while maintaining the level of job satisfaction within the department.

Some Further Good News

In view of all this, it will be clear that patent professionals will face a big challenge when they enter the intellectual capital era. Are they up to it? After all, people in general do not like change, and patent professionals are no exception. The good news is that a company like Dow has already proved to be up to it,[8] so why would it not work for other companies and their patent professionals? But, Dow is not the only successful company. Du Pont, Xerox, and Eastman Chemical, to name a few, are also making good progress, but then all these companies have the advantage that they are members of the ICM Gathering.[9] Like good news, success stories travel fast, and it will not be long before a company's CEO or the director to whom the IP director reports will ask whether in his or her company a success story like Dow's can be realized. Alternatively, a patent department may take the initiative and could start to work actively on the management of the company's intellectual assets.

Whatever way the concept will be introduced in a company, sooner or later patent professionals will have to look into the intellectual capital concept and the development and implementation of tools that enable a company to manage patent assets in an effective manner.

Preparation Is Needed

Therefore, patent professionals need to prepare themselves for the intellectual capital era, if they wish to contribute to the future success, if not survival, of their companies. This preparation is the immediate challenge a patent department has to face before it can successfully address the major challenges posed by the intellectual capital era as mentioned earlier.

To prepare themselves, patent professionals should, of course, familiarize themselves with the concept of intellectual capital. This should not be too difficult since there is an abundance of excellent literature available these days.[10] In addition, they should start experimenting with the new insights that they will gain into this field, to find out what works for their companies and what does not. It is further recommended to look into and work on the following set of integrated preparation factors:

- Vision
- Strategy
- Proactivity
- Transparency
- Flexibility
- Trust

Of course, these factors can be considered to be self-evident, but then the problem with the self-evident is that it does not get the attention it deserves; it is being taken for granted. A committed effort to work on these preparation factors will provide patent professionals a new perspective and thus their patent department the new culture it will need if it wishes to contribute to the future success of its company.

The Preparation Factors in More Detail

Vision

What is it that the patent department wishes to establish? What does it stand for? How does it fit within the company at present, and how will it fit within the company in the future? What role will it need to play to assist the company is establishing its business objectives? All very important questions, which are often easier to ask than to answer. Nonetheless, an effort should be made to answer these questions because it makes one understand the business context in which one has to work. An effective tool to use in such an effort is the preparation of a mission statement, since it will focus the department's efforts, will remind people what the role of their department is all about, what its objectives really are.

For a mission statement to be successful, all persons of the department should be actively involved in its development and all should buy into it, once it has been established.

To give an example, the mission statement of Burmah Castrol's patent department (before Burmah Castrol was taken over by BP Amoco) read as follows:

> Our aim is to be the automatic first contact for patent issues for all the Group Businesses by providing an expert, cost-effective, efficient and tailor-made patent service to each Business. This will ensure that the Businesses can take informed decisions regarding the protection and commercialization of their technologies and issues relating to Group owned patents and third party patents. In this way we will add value by securing a competitive edge for the Group locally and globally.

Strategy

How can the patent department's objectives be established? The first step is to look into each individual objective and to determine the fundamentals that are the key to success in establishing each objective or that are needed to move toward the realization of the objective in question. The resulting list of fundamentals will include a number of particular attitudes and abilities, for instance, proactivity and transparency, necessary for the patent professionals and their department to establish these objectives. In turn, these attitudes and abilities can in practice be manifested by activities. The plan of action, the selected activities, and the timing to develop these activities will be the department's strategy, which needs to be implemented. To make the strategy work, everyone within the patents department needs to be committed to its implementation.

One of the most important activities a patent department can complete is the establishment of a patent strategy for the company, or when applicable, for each business area, technology area, or individual technology.

Proactivity

The role of a patents department traditionally has been a relatively reactive one. It is expected to take action in respect of a large number of requests or demands that are dictated either by the business or by national or regional patent authorities. In view of this and the increasing workload of patent departments in general, it is usually felt that there is no time left to do useful things on top of the "daily" work, let alone to be genuinely proactive. Proactivity, however, is one of the keys to a department's future success since it can enable the department to make an effort in respect of things that really matter because they add value to the business, but that are otherwise not addressed because of lack of time. These things that really matter usually include the type of activities that would contribute to the realization of a patent department's objectives. Proactivity can be realized by improved time management[11] and more effective delegation.[12]

Activities that a proactive patents department could develop to establish its objectives could include:

- Development of a patent strategy and its implementation
- Development of a program to educate business and R&D personnel on patent matters[13]
- Development of a patents information database[14]
- Organization of annual patent assets audits
- Consideration of patent value indices and measurement indicators[15]
- Transfer of best practices by benchmarking with other companies

It is, however, important to check with business management whether these activities are aligned with their objectives before developing and implementing them and to obtain their support, because their input in the development of many of these activities is often fundamental. In addition, each individual patent professional should be expected to have a proactive approach toward possible protection and commercialization of new technology.

Transparency

Since in the future all decisions regarding patent matters will be informed business decisions, businesses will need to have ready access to all sorts of patents information. Such information will include the costs of every step in the patenting process; the costs to date of a particular patent series; and territorial coverage of a particular patent series.

To make this work, a patent department needs to be transparent to the business, and this can be realized by:

- Having open lines of communication with the business
- Having a patents information database to which the business has access
- Informing the business about the department's mission statement and its strategy
- Making sure the business knows the structure of the department
- Having clear decision-making processes in place that leave no doubts about responsibilities and accountabilities
- Informing the business about the range of services the patent department can offer and the level of service it may expect to receive
- Explaining to the business its responsibilities toward the patent department
- Developing a time-monitoring system that enables the business to understand the amount of time spent on the various patent activities

Flexibility

In times of continuous change it seems quite obvious to expect a patent department to be flexible. But what does it mean in practice and what does it require? It means that patent professionals need to learn how to adapt themselves successfully to change. This is important since many patent professionals' work includes a lot of routine tasks, especially when one has been responsible for a particular part of the patent portfolio for a number of years. Any change of their role is therefore likely to be an unsettling experience. Therefore, the sooner a patent department starts working on establishing a new internal culture the better.

Successful change can be realized by:[16]

- Communicating the reasons for change, and pointing out the opportunities
- Creating a sense of urgency[17]
- Involving all patent professionals in the change process and ensuring they buy into it
- Attending external workshops on change
- Organizing internal workshops to discuss the activities that need to be developed, as well as various aspects of intellectual asset management

- Inviting a recognized authority in the field of intellectual capital to give a presentation followed by questions and a discussion
- Releasing and making effective use of the true potential of the people within the department[18]
- Encouraging teamwork in respect of the patent portfolio management and special projects
- Encouraging patent professionals to learn more about the needs and objectives of the business, what it is that drives the business
- Generating short-term successes, for instance, by organizing patent assets audits
- Creating an atmosphere of trust
- Evaluating the change process and its progress

Trust

Trust denotes honesty, fairness, openness, and integrity, all essential ingredients that enable the creation of rich and lasting relationships within a patent department as well as with other departments within a company. It is one of the most important components to establish change in a successful manner, since it enlarges mutual understandings and common goals, resulting in an increased commitment to a patent department's success. In addition, trust enables effective teamwork and brings about a willingness to accept others' opinion and views. This is especially of importance to a patent department since patent professionals are an individualistic type of people. Trust can therefore ensure that a patent department can learn from the mistakes (and successes) of the individual patent attorneys, since it will encourage them to share experiences to the benefit of all involved. This does, of course, not only apply to a patent department internally; it should also be part of the relationship with the business. In addition, trust may encourage role-playing exercises to prepare patent professionals for court hearings or oral proceedings before a patent office. To develop trust, an atmosphere of openness should be created, wherein people have mutual respect for each other.

Conclusion

To prepare patent professionals for the intellectual capital era, a new IP culture needs to be developed and implemented. To establish this, patent professionals are advised to start working on a set of integrated preparation factors. The new IP culture will enable them to contribute to the future success of their companies. However, the foregoing does not only apply to in-house patent professionals. It also applies to patent professionals from private practice, because they also need a new IP culture that will enable them to meet the increasing demands and expectations of their clients.

Notes

1. Patrick H Sullivan, *Profiting from Intellectual Capital, Extracting Value from Innovation* (New York: John Wiley & Sons, Inc, 1998), 5.
2. Steven M. H. Wallman, "The Importance of Measuring Intangible Assets: Public Policy Implications," in *Capital for Our Time: The Economic, Legal and Management Challenges of Intellectual Capital*, ed. Nicholas Imparato (Stanford, Calif.: Hoover Institution Press, 1998), 181-91.
3. *Visualizing Intellectual Capital in Skandia.* Supplement to Skandia's 1994 annual report. This and subsequent supplements (one every six months) are assessable via the Internet. See www.Skandia-afs.com/.
4. Tim Draper, "Intellectual Capital Measurement for Start-ups: The Best of Intentions, the Worst of Outcomes," in *Capital for Our Time: The Economic, Legal and Management Challenges of Intellectual Capital*, ed. Nicholas Imparato (Stanford, Calif.: Hoover Institution Press, 1998), 233-47.
5. Sullivan, *Profiting from Intellectual Capital*, 107.
6. Sullivan, *Profiting from Intellectual Capital*, 205-20.
7. Sullivan, *Profiting from Intellectual Capital*, 335-56.
8. Conversation (in 1999) between the author and Steve Grace, Dow Chemical's general patent counsel at that time, from which it appeared that Dow's patents department's profile had risen, while at the same time work had become more interesting due to an increasing number of counseling and transactional activities.
9. For more information on the ICM Gathering, see www. ICMGroup.com.
10. See notes 1, 2, and 3. Further examples, to name a few, include: Thomas A. Stewart, *Intellectual Capital, the New Wealth of*

Organizations (London: Nicholas Brealey Publishing, 1999); Johan Roos, Göran Roos, Nicola C. Dragonetti, and Leif Edvinsson, *Intellectual Capital, Navigating the New Business Landscape* (London: MacMillan Business, 1997); *Karl Erik Sveiby, The New Organizational Wealth, Managing & Measuring Knowledge-based Assets* (San Francisco: Berrett-Koehler Publishers, Inc, 1997); Leif Edvinsson and Michael Malone, *Intellectual Capital, The Proven Way to Establish Your Company's Real Value by Measuring Its Hidden Brainpower* (London: Piatkus, 1997); Annie Brooking, I*ntellectual Capital, Core Asset for the Third Millennium Enterprise* (London: International Thomson Business Press, 1996).

11. Stephen R. Covey, *The Seven Habits of Highly Effective People* (London: Simon & Schuster Ltd, 1992); for effective time-management teachings. See also Stephen R. Covey, A. Roger Merrill, and Rebecca R. Merill, *First Things First* (London: Simon & Schuster UK Ltd., 1994).

12. David Oates, *Leadership: The Art of Delegation* (London: Century Business, 1993); for a study of delegation in general.

13. Business and R&D personnel should appreciate and understand what patents are, how they can be used to provide competitive advantage, and what the role of the patents department is within the company. It is therefore advisable to put an internal education program in place to bring all business and R&D personnel up to an acceptable base level of knowledge regarding patent rights and intellectual property rights in general. Such a program could for instance be an integral part of the induction process for all new business and R&D personnel. Also, a program of periodic reminder sessions for existing staff might prove useful.

14. A patents information database to which business and R&D personnel could have access may for instance include information on basic patent principles; list(s) of reported inventions; a blank form to report electronically a new invention; patent portfolio survey(s); third party issues; patent awareness profiles. See Sullivan, *Profiting from Intellectual Capital*, 129-41, for a discussion on the development of a portfolio database. Interestingly, it seems to suggest here that the development of such a database should emanate from the business, not the patents department, since it may otherwise receive little support. This is not necessarily the case. In Burmah Castrol, for instance, the proactive approach to developing such a patents information database has been successful.

Sveiby, Karl Erik. *The New Organizational Wealth: Managing & Measuring Knowledge-Based Assets.* San Francisco: Berrett-Koehler Publishers, Inc, 1997.

Legal Disclaimer

This book intends to provide an understanding of the elements of effective patent asset management and proposes a set of tools to establish this. The content of this book is, however, not to be considered legal advice and should therefore not be used as a substitute for professional legal advice. Consequently, the author cannot assume any responsibility for any decisions made or actions taken that are based on the content of this book.

Index

About the Author

Lex van Wijk is a Dutch and European patent attorney who has worked at Royal Dutch Shell, at Burmah Castrol as group patent manager, and at Siemens AG, where he was a member of the team responsible for coordinating and controlling the patent portfolio management activities of all the intellectual property units. He is now working at Vereenigde, where he advises clients on intellectual property matters, including patent asset management.